KRISTIN KOLSTAD ADDISON

Play Quilts

Creative Activity Quilts for Kids

Martingale™
& COMPANY

Play Quilts: Creative Activity Quilts for Kids
Kristin Kolstad Addison
© 2001 by Kristin Kolstad Addison

Martingale & Company
20205 144th Ave. NE
Woodinville, WA 98072-8478
www.martingale-pub.com

> **The quilts in this book feature small parts and are not suitable for children under the age of three.**

Credits

President • Nancy J. Martin
CEO • Daniel J. Martin
Publisher • Jane Hamada
Editorial Director • Mary V. Green
Editorial Project Manager • Tina Cook
Technical Editor • Darra Williamson
Copy Editor • Karen Koll
Design and Production Manager • Stan Green
Illustrator • Laurel Strand
Cover Designer • Stan Green
Text Designer • Trina Stahl
Photographer • Brent Kane

Mission Statement

We are dedicated to providing quality products and service by working together to inspire creativity and to enrich the lives we touch.

Printed in Hong Kong
06 05 04 03 02 01 8 7 6 5 4 3 2 1

Library of Congress Cataloging-in-Publication Data

Addison, Kristin Kolstad
    Play quilts : creative activity quilts for kids / Kristin Kolstad Addison.
        p.   cm.
    ISBN 1-56477-368-X
    1. Patchwork—Patterns.   2. Appliqué—Patterns.   3. Children's quilts.   I. Title.

TT835.A32 2001
746.46'041—dc21
                                                    2001030967

Dedication

To my three girls, Henrikke, Martine, and Karoline, who gave me ideas and creative help throughout this long project. They have been very patient during all the hours of work, even when I was in "another world," not listening and not available. Each has been promised the choice of one quilt for her own room.

Acknowledgments

WITH MANY THANKS TO:

My husband Thomas, for helping out with the computer when it crashed or something went wrong, for being my dictionary (since he is British), for drawing quilt designs, and for constant "discussions." We have several more quilts on paper, almost ready to sew. As a mining engineer, he wants a mining quilt with the Spitsbergen mines as the theme. "Lunar Landing" was also his idea, so he named it.

Henrikke, Martine, and Karoline for help, inspiration, and encouragement throughout the process, and just for being in my life.

Margaret Nygaard, a very good quilter, doll maker, and friend, for being my "quality control" and for sewing the bodies of all the dolls, leaving me to make just faces and hair. She also shared supplies, lent me inspirational books and patterns about doll making, and offered encouragement during the process of writing this book.

Contents

Introduction

THE IDEA FOR this book began when my oldest children, the twins, were almost four years old. We had just moved down to mainland Norway from Spitsbergen. There had been lots of talk about polar bears, and the children were afraid. At the same time, I was planning a bed quilt for each girl to have in their new room, and I saw a small doll pattern that I began adapting to suit my children. The ball just started to roll, faster and faster. Soon I had the quilt on paper, and I began to cut and sew. The end result was one bed-sized quilt, adorned with a dozen little dolls in mini-sleeping bags, a smiling pink-checked bear in a pocket, a campfire, and big pieced trees surrounded by lots of flowered fabric. I also attached a moon and a sun with buttons—the same way I had attached the tiny sleeping bags.

All the way, Henrikke, Martine, and soon also my youngest daughter Karoline, gave me lots of help and new ideas. Before long, the girls overcame their fear—and I had planned several new projects, of course! Then Thomas, my husband, asked, "Why not collect these ideas in a book?" And so I did.

Perhaps these quilts can help someone in a hospital or someone having fears and needing a way to "play" them out. There are no limits for how these quilts can be made, used, and loved.

Finding Your Way through This Book

BEFORE YOU BEGIN making the quilts, I'd like to explain how I designed this book. The basic information you need for making the quilts—including which tools and notions to use, as well as how to cut, stitch, quilt, and finish them—appears in the first part of the book. Then you'll find instructions and lists of required materials for making the various dolls, animals, and other moveable toys. You can choose your favorites to use on your quilt, but you'll also find a list of which toys I made for each quilt in the individual quilt instructions. The book concludes with specific instructions for each quilt.

I hope this book inspires you to make your own unique quilts for someone special in your life. That is what I want it to do!

Fabrics, Tools, and Notions

Beads: For eyes and sparkly jewels, I use colored beads. If you look closely, you'll find a big pearl in the oyster shell on the "Pirate Ship" quilt (page 63).

Buttons: There are lots of buttons on these quilts: buttons that "work" and buttons just for decoration. I use buttons of many different shapes and sizes. Apples, fish, cats, vegetables, and flowers are just a few of the fun shapes you'll see. Buttons rescued from old clothing are good, too, especially for hanging the toys on the quilts. I don't have rules about size, but find the button first and then make the loop or buttonhole to fit the button.

Always secure buttons well with extra-strong thread, such as sturdy cotton, buttonhole-twist, or even hand-quilting thread. Be aware that buttons can be very dangerous for small children, who might pull them off and swallow them. Because of the buttons, small toys, and embellishments, the quilts in this book are not appropriate for children under the age of three. Even when making quilts for children three and older, you may choose to leave buttons off and find another method for attaching dolls and toys (perhaps Velcro fastener).

Decorative trims: I use trims for doll clothes and other details. For example, the little girl doll in "Animal Train" wears a bikini made from a narrow flower-band trim, and the "Pirate Ship" mermaid sits in a ½"-wide gold-lace swing.

Fabric: I usually use cotton fabric, but I don't have any real rules about what to use and what not to use. However, since I don't like the surprise of shrinking fabric or bleeding colors, I do wash all fabric before I use it.

The choice of color is very personal, but whatever colors you choose, try to view them together at a distance to get some idea of how they will work in your quilt before you sew them together. In these quilts, I favored bright, child-friendly colors. I was always on the lookout for fun theme fabrics—such as those with grass, trees, animals, moons, and stars—to add to my collection. As a friend has said, it is always easier to combine one hundred fabrics then five or ten!

Choose a variety of different values (light to dark) when you are working on a scene with sky, sea, or grass,

or when shading from day to night as in some of the quilts in this book.

In short, have fun, and think like a child when picking fabrics, themes, and colors for these projects. Why not make a pink-checked pig?

Flannel sheet: A big flannel sheet always hangs on the wall in my workroom. It's perfect for arranging fabric pieces and blocks. You don't need to pin at all until the quilt is pretty well assembled. The nap of the flannel keeps the pieces in place.

Turn under and hem one short end of the sheet to make a sleeve. Insert a curtain rod for hanging. If for some reason you need to stop working and put aside the unfinished quilt, you can just roll the whole thing up. The pieces will be in place when you unroll it later.

Freezer paper: Freezer paper is wonderful for ironing on appliqué pieces to mark turn-under allowances or stabilize pieces for stitching. You can find it at your grocery store and in many quilt shops.

Fusible web: This paper-backed iron-on web acts as an adhesive for quick-and-easy appliqués. It comes in different brands and varieties. Experiment to find your favorite, and follow the manufacturer's instructions.

Iron: For good results, you'll need to press your work with a steam iron as you go. If you don't have a steam iron, you can use a dry iron and a spray bottle of water.

Needles: You'll need a variety of different needles for hand sewing, finishing the toys, and hand quilting. Be sure to choose a size that is comfortable in your hand and appropriate for the thread you are using.

An appliqué needle is ideal for most of your sewing needs. It is long, fine, and very sharp. You'll probably find that some threads are easier to thread directly from the spool, while others pass more smoothly through the needle's eye from the cut end. If you find it difficult to thread the needle, try licking the eye of the needle instead of the thread.

A special needle called a Between makes it easier to get tiny, consistent hand-quilting stitches. These needles come in a variety of different sizes (usually 5–12), with the higher numbers indicating the smallest needle sizes.

Use a long, sharp wool-embroidery needle to add details such as eyes and mouths to the doll faces. You can also use these needles for attaching the dolls' hair.

Pencils: An ordinary pencil with fairly soft lead is good for marking fabric and making templates. When applied lightly, it washes away, and you can often even erase it from the fabric if you need to.

Permanent markers and pens: I sometimes use a fine-point permanent marker or pen for drawing faces on dolls and toys. They are also useful when making labels for finished work.

Pins: I prefer to use long quilter's pins with large plastic heads. They're easy to see, and they hold all the quilt layers securely.

Rotary cutter, mat, and ruler: A rotary cutter and mat are invaluable for accurate cutting. An 18" x 24" mat is roomy enough to cut all the pieces you'll need for these quilts, dolls, and toys.

I prefer to use a 4" square ruler for cutting fabric, especially when cutting tiny pieces. I use a larger ruler (6" x 24") when strip piecing and for cutting very large pieces, such as borders. I also use the larger ruler, and a rotary cutter with a spare (utility) blade, for cutting large pieces of paper and cardboard. Using the rotary cutter is quicker and more accurate than using scissors.

Be sure your rulers are marked in ⅛" intervals. If they are slippery, glue small sandpaper circles on the back to keep the rulers steady as you work.

Satin ribbon: I use narrow satin ribbon for many details: in matching colors to make hanging loops for toys, to tie doll hair, to hang a hammock in the tree in "On the Farm" (page 74), and to link the wagons on the "Animal Train" (page 89). I use it in doll clothes for belts, waistbands and neckbands, arm loops and shoulder straps, and for other decoration.

Always check for color bleeding before using *any* ribbon. Soak the ribbon thoroughly and lay it to dry between two layers of white cotton fabric. If the fabric is still white and shows no trace of color, the ribbon should be safe to use.

Scissors: You'll want a good pair of dressmaker's scissors to use exclusively for cutting fabric and sturdy utility scissors for cutting cardboard, template plastic, and paper. A pair of small, sharp, pointed scissors is useful for appliqué, and also for clipping corners and seams.

Seam ripper: This tool always comes in handy.

Sewing machine and accessories: You'll need a machine capable of a reliable straight stitch and basic zigzag stitch for assembling the quilts, dolls, and toys in this book. A walking foot makes machine quilting straight lines easier, and a darning or embroidery foot makes free-motion quilting fun and easy. Be sure the needle is sharp and sized correctly for the task and the fabric.

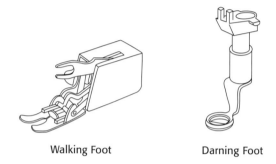

Walking Foot   Darning Foot

Template materials: Shirt cardboard or oaktag works well. It's not too thick, but it's sturdier than paper. Plastic or Mylar sheets sold especially for quilters are flexible, and perfect for cutting nice, smooth curves.

Thread: Since the toys are intended for active play, I use strong polyester thread for stitching their seams.

When machine quilting, I use ordinary polyester sewing thread, cotton or silk hand-quilting thread, or Sulky machine-embroidery thread. Each gives a completely different result. Ordinary sewing thread practically disappears in the quilt, while hand-quilting thread is the most visible. Sulky embroidery thread gives a wonderful, shiny look, but be careful not to soak the quilt for prolonged periods, or the lustrous thread might bleed onto the surrounding fabric.

When machine quilting, I use ordinary sewing thread in the bobbin in a color to match the quilt backing. If I can't match the color exactly, I use a slightly darker—rather than lighter—shade.

For making and attaching doll hair, I use thin wool yarn in yellow, brown, black, or red. I select embroidery thread or wool yarn of similar weight in blue, green, or brown for embroidering eyes, and pink or different shades of red for stitching mouths.

Basic Quiltmaking Techniques

Rotary Cutting

INSTRUCTIONS FOR quick-and-easy rotary cutting are provided wherever possible. Measurements for all rotary cut strips and pieces include ¼"-wide seam allowances.

Cutting Accurate Strips

1. Fold the fabric selvage to selvage, aligning the crosswise and lengthwise grains as much as possible. Place the folded edge closest to you on the cutting mat, and align one edge of a square ruler with the fold. Place a long, straight ruler to the left of the square, just covering the uneven raw edges on the left side of the fabric.

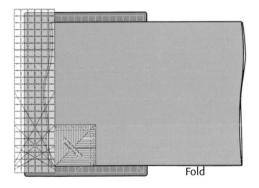

Fold

2. Remove the square ruler and use your rotary cutter to cut along the right edge of the long ruler. Discard this fabric strip. (Reverse this procedure if you are left-handed.)

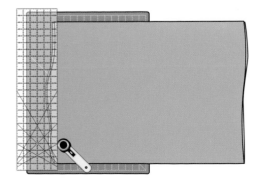

3. Align the newly cut edge of the fabric with the ruler marking at the required measurement. For example, to cut a 3"-wide strip, place the 3" ruler marking on the edge of the fabric.

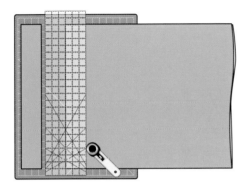

4. To cut squares, cut strips in the required widths and use a small, square ruler to measure and crosscut the strips into squares. The side measurement of each square should equal the width of the strip. Continue cutting squares until you have the number needed.

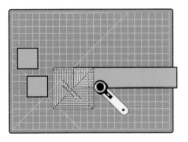

5. To cut half-square triangles, cut a square ⅞" larger than the finished size of the short side of the triangle. Cut the square once diagonally from corner to corner. Each square yields 2 triangles with the short sides on the straight grain of the fabric.

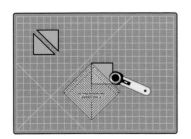

6. To cut quarter-square triangles, cut a square 1¼" larger than the finished size of the long edge of the triangle. Cut the square twice diagonally, from corner to corner. Each square yields 4 triangles with the long side on the straight grain of the fabric.

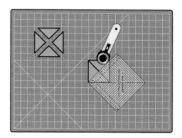

7. To cut bias strips, fold and trim the fabric as described in steps 1 and 2. Align the 45° line on the ruler with the cut edge, and then cut along the ruler's long edge. The cut edge will be a bias edge. Align the newly cut bias edge of the fabric with the ruler marking at the required measurement, and cut bias strips as needed.

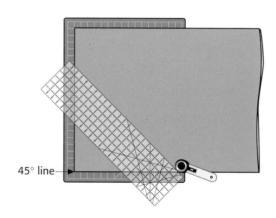

45° line

Using Templates

MOST OF the dolls, animals, moveable toys, and flat pieces are cut using full-sized patterns. So are some of the pieces used in constructing the quilts themselves. All patterns are included in this book.

Unless otherwise noted, the patterns for dolls, doll clothes, animals, and toys *do not* include seam allowances. The directions for these items specify how to deal with seam allowances.

Unless otherwise noted, patterns for quilt pieces *do* include ¼"-wide seam allowances. (Appliqué patterns do not, and you will be instructed how to handle these—depending upon the appliqué method used—in the

specific directions.) When grain line matters, patterns are marked with grain line arrows to indicate the correct placement of the template on the fabric.

Make the templates, trace, and cut the fabric as instructed in the specific project instructions.

Quick Chain Piecing

THIS QUICK-PIECING machine technique saves you time and thread.

1. Set the stitch length on your sewing machine to approximately 12 to 15 stitches per inch; that is, small enough to stitch secure seams, but not so small as to resist a seam ripper.

2. Beginning with a "thread saver" (a small scrap of leftover fabric), sew the first pair of pieces, right sides together, from cut edge to cut edge. At the end of the seam, stop sewing, but do not cut the thread.

3. Feed the next pair of pieces under the presser foot, as close as possible to the first. Continue feeding pieces through the machine, without stopping to cut the threads or backstitch between the pairs. Finish the chain with another thread saver, and clip the thread tail to free it from the machine.

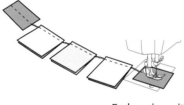

End sewing with
a thread saver.

4. If the complete unit consists of just these two pieces, clip the threads between the stitched units and press as directed in the quilt instructions. If you will be adding another piece to the stitched units, don't clip the threads. Instead, clip a thread saver from the first chain and reuse it to start another row, adding the new piece to the previous chain, as described in step 3 and illustrated below.

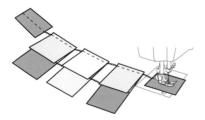

5. Continue adding pieces, chaining but not clipping threads except to start a new row.

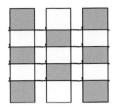

6. When all rows are complete, press the seams in opposite directions from row to row. Pinning carefully to match the seams, sew the rows together. Ease slightly if necessary, and press.

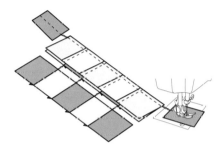

Pressing

YOU'LL WANT to press your piecework carefully to minimize bulky seams and to finish with a nice, flat quilt top. I recommend which way to press the seam allowances in the text and illustrations for each quilt project.

Fusible Appliqué

THERE ARE so many ways to appliqué, and everybody has a favorite method. Fusible appliqué is very quick and easy! I used it to attach the starfish on the "Pirate Ship" quilt. To try this technique, you'll need a fusible web, such as Wonder Under (see page 7).

1. Trace the appliqué pattern on the paper side of the fusible web. Cut out the shape, adding a generous margin around the drawn line, and iron it, web side down, to the wrong side of the appliqué fabric.

2. Cut out the fabric shape directly on the drawn line.

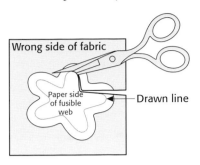

3. Remove the paper and place the appliqué, right side up, where you want it to appear on the quilt. Follow the manufacturer's instructions to iron the appliqué in place. Stitch around the outer edges of the shape with quilting or embroidery thread in a buttonhole stitch to finish.

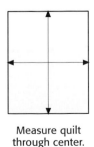

Buttonhole Stitch

Adding Borders

BORDERS ADD a finishing touch, acting as a colorful frame for the quilt. Cutting measurements are given for each quilt, but it's always a good idea to measure your own quilt before cutting the border strips. You may discover some slight variations in the size of your quilt top. These differences often occur as the quilt is handled, sewn, and pressed.

Always measure the quilt top through the center in both directions when determining how long to cut border strips. That way, you are sure you are cutting the

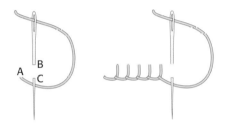

Measure quilt through center.

borders to fit the quilt, and not vice versa. Borders on opposite sides of the quilt should measure exactly the same in order to get perfect 90° corners and a quilt that finishes as a true rectangle or square.

Straight-Cut Borders

1. Measure the width of the quilt top through the center. Cut 2 strips from the crosswise grain of the border fabric to that measurement, piecing them as necessary to get the desired length. Mark the center of the quilt edges and the border strips. Pin the border strips to the top and bottom of the quilt, matching center marks and ends and easing as necessary. Sew the border strips to the quilt, and press seams toward the borders.

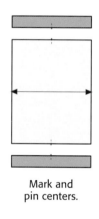

Mark and
pin centers.

2. Measure the length of the quilt top through the center, including the top and bottom borders just added. From the crosswise grain of the remaining border fabric, cut 2 border strips to that measurement, piecing as necessary. Mark the center of the quilt edges and the border strips. Pin the borders to the side edges of the quilt, matching center marks, seams, and ends, and easing as necessary. Sew the border strips to the quilt, and press the seams toward the borders.

If the quilt has multiple borders, finish adding one set before starting on the next.

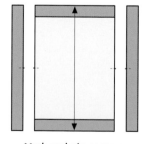

Mark and pin centers.

Backing and Batting

Note: *For wall hangings or bed-sized quilts, cut the backing and batting at least 2" larger than the quilt top on all sides. Whenever possible, especially for wall hangings, run the lengthwise grain of the backing fabric vertically (top to bottom).*

CHOOSE AND prewash good-quality fabric to use for the back of your quilt. The backing should last as long as the top! It's fun to find backing material that matches the theme of the quilt and fits the quilting patterns you choose.

If you need to, you can sew several lengths of different fabrics together for a more personal and fun—as well as a larger—quilt backing.

The choice of batting is more important than most people realize. Don't ruin a wonderful quilt with inferior batting. Think of all the work we put into our quilts! I prefer good-quality, light cotton or wool batting. Then I am sure the quilt will become more and more beautiful as the years go by.

Explore a bit before making your final selection. There are so many types and thicknesses on the market; you'll surely find batting suitable for your project.

I never throw away any of the batting leftovers, because they are so handy. I use leftover wool batting for small, stuffed toy parts and leftover cotton for all flat toys and pieces that require a filler.

Basting

To PREVENT wrinkles and bumps in the finished quilt, it is important that the layers of your quilt (top, batting, and backing) be secured together for quilting. This is especially true when machine quilting.

Spray Basting

Recently I've started basting my quilts with a spray basting adhesive. It has shown me a whole new world! I used to baste my quilts by hand with needle and thread. Now, working in a well-ventilated area, I just spray adhesive on top of the batting and roll the quilt top over it, smoothing as I go. Then I flip the sandwich over and do the same for the backing. The spray works so well that an extremely thin layer is enough, and if I need to reposition the quilt top or backing, I simply lift off the layer I need to reposition and do so. No additional spray is needed.

Thread Basting

If spray adhesive is not available, or if you prefer, baste your quilt by hand. A long (7") dollmaker's needle comes in handy for this task. Layer the backing (wrong side up) and the batting, and then center the quilt top (right side up) over the two. Starting from the center of the quilt sandwich, baste along the diagonals with long stitches. Continue by basting in a horizontal and vertical grid, with lines of stitching no more than 7" apart, and working from the center of the quilt outwards.

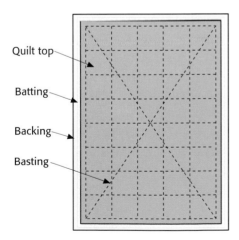

Quilt top
Batting
Backing
Basting

Safety-Pin Basting

Safety-pin basting is quicker than thread basting. Choose rustproof pins that are large enough to hold all three layers. (There are even safety pins made especially for basting!) Start pinning in the center of the quilt and work outwards, placing pins about 5" apart.

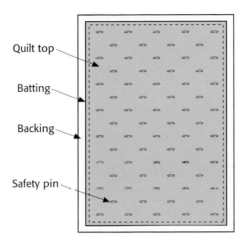

Quilt top
Batting
Backing
Safety pin

Quilting
Marking for Quilting

If you are planning to hand quilt, you will probably want to mark the desired quilt pattern on the quilt top. There are many different quilting patterns available in premade plastic stencils. These stencils have a cut line to follow and are perfect for tracing repeating patterns. Use a pencil or other removable marking tool to trace the desired pattern lightly, remembering to test your marking tool on a scrap of fabric to be sure that you can remove it when the quilting is finished.

Pre-marked patterns can be difficult to follow when machine quilting because of the speed required for smooth, machine-quilted curves. Instead, appreciate that machine quilting is a completely different technique than hand quilting, and don't try to make it look the same. Think "scribble" or "doodle" when machine quilting, and emphasize the difference for more free-spirited results.

Hand Quilting

For hand quilting, you'll need short, sturdy quilting needles (called Betweens), quilting thread, a pair of small scissors for clipping threads, and at least one thimble. I use two "tape-on" thimbles—one for each hand.

1. Thread the needle with a single strand of quilting thread about 18" long. Make a small knot at the end of the thread. Insert the needle in the top layer about 1" away from the place where you want to start stitching. Pull the needle out at the point where the quilting will begin, and gently tug on the thread until the knot pops through the fabric into the batting.

2. Take a tiny backstitch, and start quilting by rocking the needle up and down to take small, evenly spaced stitches through all quilt layers. For the best results, try to take 3 or 4 stitches on the needle before pulling the needle through. Aim for about 7 stitches per inch.

3. To end a line of quilting (or as you are reaching the end of the thread), make a small knot close to the last stitch. Take another tiny back stitch, running the thread a needle's length through the batting. Gently pull the thread until the knot pops into the batting, and clip the thread at the quilt's surface.

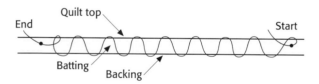

Machine Quilting

Machine quilting is suitable for all types of quilts, from wall hangings to full-size bed quilts. With a little practice, you can achieve beautiful results, and the process is fast and fun.

For straight-line quilting, it is helpful to use a walking foot (see page 8). This special foot attachment helps feed all three layers through the machine without shifting and puckering, and it helps you to get even, consistent stitches.

For free-motion quilting, use a darning-foot attachment (see page 8) and lower the feed dogs on your machine. This allows you to move the quilt freely in any direction, making it possible to outline-quilt a fabric motif or create stippling, doodles, or other curved designs. You can even write words on your quilt!

To start and stop a line of machine quilting, draw the bobbin thread up to the top layer of the quilt and make five or six tiny stitches in place to secure the thread. Adjust the stitch to the desired length and feed the quilt sandwich under the needle, maintaining a consistent, medium to high speed. Don't push or pull the fabric as you stitch, as this will result in uneven stitches and may cause you to break the needle.

It's a good idea to practice a little before stitching on your quilt. Fold a piece of fabric and place a piece of batting between the two layers to make a sandwich. Practice stitching smooth curves. Quilt your name. Try stipple quilting, which is very much like scribbling with a pen on paper.

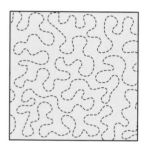 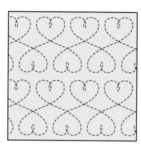

Free-Motion Quilting

Tip

Just before you are ready to start quilting, try sketching your intended quilting pattern on a piece of paper. This helps to get the movements in your hand and head.

Adding a Hanging Sleeve

IF YOU plan to display your finished quilt on the wall, be sure to add a hanging sleeve to hold the rod. If you choose to add a hanging sleeve, you will trim your batting and backing before you add the quilt binding instead of after.

Cut a piece of fabric 6" to 8" wide x the width of the quilt minus 2". Turn the short ends under ¼", then ¼" again and stitch. Fold the fabric strip in half lengthwise, wrong sides together, and press. Trim the batting and backing even with the quilt top. Center the sleeve on the top back edge of the quilt, aligning the raw edges, and pin. The sleeve will be secured when the binding is attached. When the binding is completed, blindstitch the sleeve's folded edge to the back of the quilt, allowing a little "give" to accommodate the thickness of the rod.

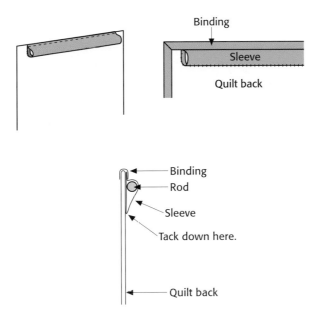

Binding

I ALMOST always use a straight-grain, double-fold binding on my quilts. It gives the quilt an elegant and durable finishing touch. Depending on the size of the quilt and how wide I want the finished binding to be, I cut my strips from 2" to 3" wide. When folded and stitched, these measurements yield finished bindings from 3/8" to 5/8". I use a 1/4" quilter's foot to sew on the narrowest bindings. For wider bindings, I use a larger foot or sew 3/8" from the raw edge.

To find the total length of binding you'll need, total the measurements of all sides of your quilt and add about 10" for corners and seams. Cut the necessary number of strips in the width of your choice from the crosswise grain (selvage to selvage) of the binding fabric.

To determine how many strips you'll need, measure the width of the binding fabric and divide the total inches of binding needed by the fabric width. (Don't forget to add that extra 10"!)

Follow these easy instructions to make and add the binding:

1. With right sides together, join strips at right angles and stitch across the corner as shown. Trim excess fabric and press the seams open to make 1 long piece of binding.

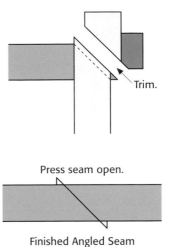

2. Trim one end of the strip at a 45° angle, turn under, and press. Fold the strip in half lengthwise, wrong sides together, and press.

3. Starting on one side of the quilt (not a corner) and using a 1/4"-wide seam allowance (or 3/8" for wider bindings), stitch the binding to the quilt, right sides together and keeping the raw edges of the binding even with the raw edges of the quilt top. Begin the stitching approximately 1" from the start of the binding and sew all the way to the first corner.

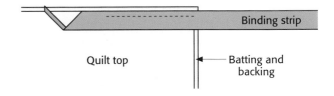

4. Without cutting the thread, lift the needle and presser foot and pivot the quilt so that you can begin stitching the binding to the adjacent side. Fold the binding up, away from the quilt, with the raw edges of the binding and quilt top aligned.

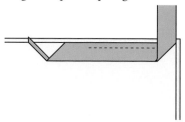

5. Fold the binding back down onto itself, even with the edge of the quilt top, and pin. Begin stitching at the top edge of the binding, once again taking a ¼"- (or ⅜"-) wide seam allowance.

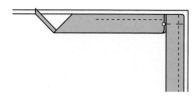

6. Repeat the process on the remaining edges and corners of the quilt. When you reach the starting point of the binding, stop stitching. Overlap the starting end of the binding by about 1" and cut away any excess. Tuck the end of the binding into the fold and finish the seam.

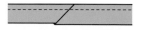

7. Trim the excess batting and backing even with the edges of the quilt top. Fold the binding over the raw edges to the back of the quilt with the folded edge covering the row of machine stitching. Blindstitch the binding in place with thread to match the binding color. A miter will form at each corner. Blindstitch the mitered corners in place.

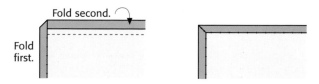

Fold second.

Fold first.

Signing Your Quilt

ONE DAY someone somewhere will wonder: who made this quilt, when, and for whom?

Try to develop the good habit of signing your quilts. Labels can be as simple or as fancy as you wish. You can use a leftover block, an extra toy, a piece of fun fabric, or a preprinted fabric made especially for labeling. Use a permanent pen to record the important information: name of the quilt, your name, your city and state (or country), the date, the name of the recipient if it is a gift, and any other important or interesting information about the quilt.

In addition to fancy decorative stitches, many sewing machines are programmed to embroider letters and numbers. Why not use that function to create your label? I sometimes use my Husqvarna Viking Designer 1 to embroider label information right on the quilt top, as a decorative element, before I baste it.

The Dolls and Toys

THE QUILTS IN this book include lots of dolls and animals placed in various pockets or loops on the quilts. You'll also find lots of animals and toys with loops that attach to the quilt with buttons. Instructions for making the individual doll and toy figures are included here.

Instructions for all fixed items or pieces are included with the directions for the specific quilt they are a part of.

I use a ¼" foot on my machine for sewing all dolls, clothes, and toys. Unless otherwise noted, use ¼" seams throughout.

> **Note:** *Unless otherwise noted, the drawn line (solid line on the pattern) is the sewing line for all dolls and toys.*

Dolls

You'll need: scrap of unbleached muslin or fabric of your choice for skin (approximately 6" x 12"); batting scraps or stuffing; yarn for hair; seed beads, embroidery floss, and/or fine-point permanent pen for facial features; fabric and trimmings for clothing.

Basic Doll Body

1. Trace the basic doll pattern (page 28) onto your preferred template material. Cut out the template.

2. Fold the piece of fabric for the doll body (skin) in half crosswise, right sides together, and place the template on the fabric, noting the grain-line markings. Trace around the template with a sharp pencil, but *do not cut the fabric.*

3. Set your sewing machine for a very small stitch (e.g., 20 stitches per inch). Machine stitch on the drawn line, leaving an opening as indicated on the pattern for turning. Sew a second time to reinforce the doll for vigorous play. Cut out the figure, adding a ¼"-wide seam allowance. Clip or notch all curves.

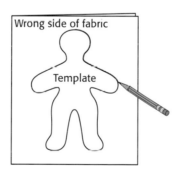

4. Turn the figure right side out. Stuff the arms and legs with small tufts of batting; then add larger tufts for the head. Add additional stuffing to the body until the entire figure is well filled. (The stuffing will soften a bit as the figure is handled.)

5. Close the opening by hand with a blind or ladder stitch in matching thread. If you wish, hand stitch from shoulder to armpit on each arm. The arms will bend more easily for dressing.

Doll Hair

Use a cardboard wig frame to make the hair for the various dolls. For long hair, cut a 7" x 5" rectangle from sturdy cardboard. Cut a second, 2½" x 3½" rectangle in the center of the large rectangle, and mark the center point on both long outer edges.

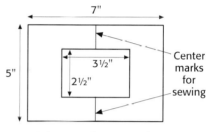

Wig Frame for Long Hair

For short hair, cut a 2" x 5" rectangle of cardboard. Cut a second, 1½" x 2½" rectangle in the center of the larger rectangle, and mark the center point on both short outer edges.

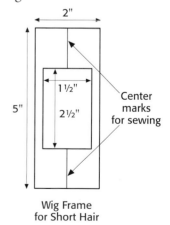

Wig Frame
for Short Hair

Wrap colored yarn around the preferred wig frame, spanning the sides opposite the center markings as shown on page 18. Continue wrapping until the yarn reaches the desired thickness. Using the marked center points as a guide, machine stitch back and forth across the yarn several times with a sturdy, matching cotton thread. Cut the yarn at both ends as shown.

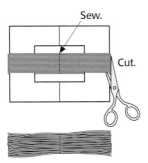

Finished Hairpiece

To attach the hair, center the front edge of the newly made hairpiece approximately ½" in front of the head seam and pin it in place. Trim short bangs on the front side if desired.

Starting from the front edge and working toward the back, use wool thread to match the wig and small hand stitches to secure the hairpiece to the head along the center part. Make additional stitches to attach the hair around the face and the back of the head.

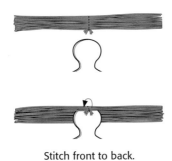

Stitch front to back.

Stitch.

Long hair may be braided or tied into a ponytail. Short hair should be left a bit untidy.

Doll Faces

Use embroidery thread and small, straight stitches and/or French knots to embroider the eyes, nose, and mouth on each doll (see suggestions on page 28). If you prefer, substitute seed beads for the eyes, draw all of the features with fine-point, permanent-ink pens, or combine the various techniques.

Individual Dolls

Each of the quilts includes its own variations on the basic doll. I have included the instructions for the different dolls here (mentioning the quilt it goes with) in case you want to switch a doll or make a doll by itself as a separate treat for someone special!

Moon People ("Lunar Landing")

For each doll, you'll need: fabric and stuffing for basic doll (page 17), 3 seed beads for eyes and navel.

Make a basic doll for each figure (page 17), adding 2 seed beads for eyes and 1 for a navel.

Pilot Girl and Boy ("Lunar Landing")

For each doll, you'll need supplies for basic doll (page 17), scrap of white silk or cotton and 1" strip of ¼"-wide Velcro fastener for coveralls, embroidery floss for initials (optional).

Make a basic doll for each figure (page 17), adding hair and face as desired. Each pilot is dressed in white coveralls. For each pair:

1. Trace the coveralls pattern (page 29) onto your preferred template material. Cut out the template.

2. Fold a scrap of white silk or cotton right sides together. Place the template on the fabric, taking careful note of the grain-line

markings, and trace around the template with a sharp pencil. Cut, adding a ¼"-wide seam allowance. Trace and cut 2 units. Each unit yields both a regular and a reverse piece.

3. Pin a regular and a reverse piece right sides together and sew the seam on the drawn line from neck to crotch to complete the front of the coveralls; repeat for the back. Unfold the sewn pairs and press the seams open.

Make 2.

4. Pin the front and back pieces right sides together and sew on the drawn line from sleeve to sleeve as shown. Clip and notch all curves.

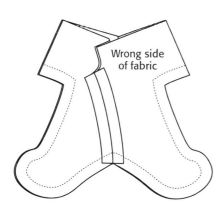

5. Hand or machine sew a ¼"-wide hem at each wrist and on the front and back necklines. Sew 1 shoulder from the wrist to the neckline, leaving the other shoulder open. Turn the garment right side out.

6. Fold a ¼"-wide hem to the wrong side on the unsewn shoulder (front and back), along what would have been the shoulder seam. Sew a ¼" x 1" strip of Velcro fastener on top of the folded hem on both the front and back shoulder.

7. If desired, hand embroider the initials of the pilot on the coverall. Dress the doll to finish.

Pirate ("Pirate Ship")

You'll need: supplies for basic doll (page 17), scrap of black cotton for shorts, scrap of white cotton knit fabric for tank top, scrap of black felt and scrap of fine black elastic for eye patch, scrap of red silk for head scarf.

Make a basic doll (page 17), adding hair and face as desired. The pirate is dressed in black shorts, a white tank top, an eye patch, and a red head scarf.

1. Trace the shorts and tank top patterns (page 28) onto your preferred template material. Cut out the template.

2. To make the shorts, fold a scrap of black cotton right sides together. Place the shorts template on the fabric, noting the grain-line markings. Trace around the template with a sharp pencil. Cut, adding a ¼" seam allowance.

3. Hand or machine stitch a ¼"-wide hem on each leg.

4. Pin the pieces right sides together and sew the center front and back seams as shown. Clip or notch all curves. Match the center front and back seams and sew the inseam as shown.

5. Hand stitch a ¼"-wide hem at the waistline. Turn the garment right side out.

6. To make the tank top, fold a scrap of white cotton knit fabric right sides together. Place the tank top template on the fabric, noting the grain-line markings. Trace around the template with a sharp pencil and cut, adding a ¼"-wide seam allowance.

7. Pin the front and back pieces right sides together and sew the shoulder and side seams on the drawn lines, leaving the arm-holes open.

Wrong side of fabric

8. Hand stitch a ¼"-wide hem at the neckline, each armhole, and the bottom edge of the shirt. Turn the garment right side out and dress the doll.

9. To make the eye patch, cut a tiny circle (⅓" diameter) of black felt. Stitch through the felt with a 5" length of fine black elastic. Place the patch over 1 eye, and knot the elastic on the back of the pirate's head.

10. Cut a 4" x 4" square of red silk to make the head scarf. Fold the raw edges to the wrong side ¼", and then ¼" again, and sew with tiny zigzag stitches in matching thread. Pinch each corner and stitch to make a knot. Place the scarf on the

pirate's head and knot adjacent corners so the scarf forms a "hat."

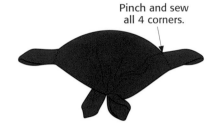

Pinch and sew all 4 corners.

11. If you wish, use a fine-point, permanent fabric pen to give the pirate a few tattoos!

Little Girl in the Red Dress ("Pirate Ship")

You'll need: supplies for basic doll (page 17), scrap of red-print fabric and 6" piece of narrow white lace or trim for dress, 4" length of 2"-wide ungathered eyelet for underpants.

Make a basic doll (page 17), adding hair and face as desired. This little girl wears a red, lace-edged dress and tiny eyelet underpants.

1. Trace the dress pattern (page 28) onto your preferred template material. Cut out the template.

2. To make the dress, fold a scrap of red-print fabric right sides

together. Place the dress template on the fabric, noting the grain-line markings. Trace around the template with a sharp pencil and cut, adding a ¼"-wide seam allowance.

3. Pin the front and back pieces right sides together and sew the shoulder seams on the drawn lines. Press the seams open. Stitch a ¼"-wide hem at each wrist. Sew the underarm and side seams. Clip and notch all curves, and hem the bottom of the dress. Turn the garment right side out and stitch the narrow lace or trim to the bottom hem.

4. Fold a ¼"-wide hem to the wrong side of the neckline. Beginning at the center front, hem the neckline with a strong gathering thread. Be sure to leave a long knotted tail on the dress front at both the starting and finishing ends so the neck-line may be loosened and tight-ened to dress the doll.

5. Use the 4" length of 2"-wide ungathered eyelet to make underpants. Stitch a ¼"-wide zigzag hem on the long straight edge to finish the waistline.

6. Fold the hemmed strip right sides together, matching the short raw edges; stitch. Center this seam, press it open, and turn the garment right side out.

Wrong side of eyelet

7. Take a few small stitches through all layers at the center point as shown to make individual leg holes. Dress the doll to finish.

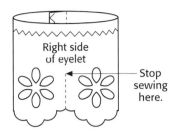

Right side of eyelet

← Stop sewing here.

Little Boy ("Pirate Ship")

You'll need: supplies for basic doll (page 17), scraps of 2 different blue homespun plaids or checks for shirt and pants.

Make a basic doll (page 17), adding hair and face as desired. This little boy wears a shirt and pants cut from blue homespun fabrics.

1. Trace the shirt/blouse and pants patterns (page 28) onto your preferred template material. Cut out the templates.

2. Following the instructions for making the pirate, steps 2 through 5 (page 19), use a folded scrap of blue homespun plaid/check to cut and assemble the full-length pants.

3. To make the shirt, fold a scrap of blue homespun plaid/check right sides together. Place the shirt/blouse template on the fabric, noting the grain-line markings. Trace around the template with a sharp pencil and cut, adding a ¼"-wide seam allowance.

4. Stitch a ¼"-wide hem at the neckline, wrist, and bottom of each piece.

5. Pin the front and back pieces right sides together and sew the shoulder seams on the drawn line; press the seams open. Sew the underarm and side seams. Clip and notch all curves and turn the garment right side out. Dress the doll to finish.

Mermaid ("Pirate Ship")

You'll need: scraps of fabric of your choice for skin and blue or green mottled-print fabric for tail; batting scraps or stuffing; yarn for hair; seed beads, embroidery floss, and/or fine-point permanent pen for facial features; scrap of flower or lace trim for bikini top; seed bead for navel; small bead necklace (or beads and fine elastic to string your own).

1. Trace the mermaid top and tail patterns (page 29) onto your preferred template material. Cut out the template.

2. Fold a scrap of fabric for skin right sides together. Place the mermaid top template on the fabric, noting the grain-line markings. Trace around the template with a sharp pencil and cut, adding a ¼"-wide seam allowance. Repeat, substituting a blue or green fabric and the mermaid tail pattern for the bottom half of the mermaid doll.

3. Set your sewing machine for a small stitch (e.g., 20 stitches per inch). With right sides together, sew a mermaid top to each mermaid tail at the waist, sewing on the drawn line.

4. With right sides together, sew together top-and-tail units from step 3. Leave an opening in the tail for turning as indicated on the pattern. Clip or notch all curves.

5. Complete the doll by following the basic doll body instructions, steps 4 and 5, on pages 17. Add face and hair as desired.

6. Trim and hand stitch the scrap of lace or flower trim to the mermaid for the bikini top. Add a seed-bead navel, and place a small beaded necklace around the mermaid's neck to finish.

Farm Girl and Farm Boy ("On the Farm")

For each doll, you'll need: supplies for basic doll (page 17). For the farm girl, you'll also need: scrap of yellow-checked cotton; 8" strip of ½"-wide yellow satin ribbon; two 2½" pieces of ¼"-wide elastic; 2 small, decorative buttons; small red "utility" button for the overalls. For the farm boy, you'll also need: scrap of red-checked cotton for the pants, blue felt (and optional fabric glue) for the vest.

Make a basic doll (page 17) for each figure, adding face and hair as desired. The farm girl is dressed in yellow-checked bib overalls, and the farm boy wears red-checked pants and a blue felt vest.

1. To make the overalls, trace the overalls pattern (page 29) onto your preferred template material. Cut out the template.

2. Fold a scrap of yellow-checked cotton right sides together. Place the overalls template on the fabric, noting the grain-line markings. Trace around the template with a sharp pencil and cut, adding a ¼"-wide seam allowance.

3. With right sides together, sew the center front and back overall seams with a ¼"-wide seam allowance. Clip or notch all curves, and press the seams to one side.

4. Machine stitch a double ¼"-wide hem on each overall leg.

Wrong side of fabric

5. Fold the overalls so the front and back seams are centered over each other. Sew the crotch seam with a ¼"-wide seam allowance as shown. Clip or notch the seam allowance and press the seam to one side.

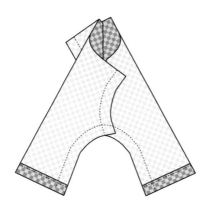

6. Turn the garment right side out. Fold the ½"-wide yellow satin ribbon over the top edge of the bib front and along the armholes to the back, trim as necessary, and stitch in place with matching thread.

7. Stitch one end of each 2½" elastic strip to a corner of the bib front and the other end to the back of the garment, crossing them over as shown.

8. Refer to the photo on page 22. Complete the garment with decorative buttons on the bib front, and add a "utility" button (for show only) on the back. Dress the farm girl doll. Roll up the overall legs, if desired.

9. For the pants and vest, trace the pants pattern (page 28) and vest pattern (page 29) onto your preferred template material. Cut out the templates. Follow the instructions for making the pirate, steps 2 through 5 (page 19), using a scrap of red-checked cotton to cut and assemble the *full-length* pants.

10. To make the vest, place the vest template on a scrap of blue felt. Trace around the template with a sharp pencil and *cut on the drawn lines.*

11. Glue or stitch the shoulder seams. Dress the doll to finish.

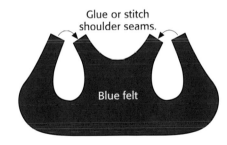
Glue or stitch shoulder seams.
Blue felt

Train Boy and Girl ("Animal Train")

For each doll, you'll need: supplies for basic doll (page 17). For the train boy, you'll also need: scrap of shiny black silk for the pants, black felt (and optional fabric glue) for the vest. For the train girl, you'll also need: one 3", one 2¼", and one 1½" strip of ¼"-wide elastic for the bikini; one 2", one 2½", and one 1¼" strip of ½"-wide flowered trim for the bikini; scrap of yellow-checked cotton and 5" strip of ½"-wide lace or trim for the robe; optional scrap of beaded trim for "scrunchee."

Make a basic doll (page 17) for each figure, adding face and hair as desired. The train boy wears black pants and a black felt vest. The train girl wears a flowered bikini and yellow-checked robe.

1. For the pants and vest, trace the pants pattern (page 28) and vest pattern (page 29) onto your preferred template material. Cut out the templates. Follow the instructions for making the pirate, steps 2 through 5 (page 19), using the black silk to make the *full-length* pants.

2. Using the scrap of black felt, follow steps 10 and 11 (left) to make the vest.

3. For the bikini top, make a loop of the 3" elastic strip and sew it with a machine zigzag to the center point of the 2" strip of flowered trim. Sew one end of the 2¼" elastic strip to each end of the flowered trim to finish.

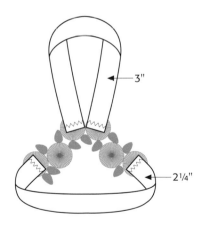
3"
2¼"

4. To make the bikini bottom, machine zigzag one end of the 1½" elastic strip to each end of the 2½" strip of flowered trim. Find the center point of both the trim and the elastic, and sew one end of the 1¼" flowered trim strip to each center point.

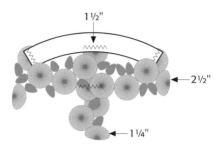

5. To make the robe, trace the robe/dress front and back patterns (page 29) onto your preferred template material. Cut out the templates.

6. Fold a scrap of yellow-checked cotton right sides together. Place the robe/dress front template on the fabric, noting the grain-line markings. Trace around the template with a sharp pencil and cut, adding a ¼"-wide seam allowance. You'll now have both the left and right robe fronts.

7. Unfold the scrap and place the robe/dress back template on the fabric, once again noting the grain line. Trace around the template with a sharp pencil and cut, adding a ¼"-wide seam allowance.

8. Pin each front piece right sides together with the back piece, aligning the side seams. Sew both shoulder seams on the drawn line; then hem the neckline, sleeves, and front edge of the robe with a ¼"-wide hem.

9. Sew both underarm and side seams. Clip or notch all curves, and hem the bottom of the robe.

10. Turn the garment right side out, and stitch the ½"-wide lace or trim to the bottom hem. Dress the doll, and—if you wish—style her hair with a "scrunchee" made from a scrap of beaded, elasticized trim.

Sleepover Girl #1 ("Sleepover Picnic")

You'll need: supplies for basic doll (page 17), 5" strip of 1"-wide blue-and-white checked ribbon and a tiny scrap of Velcro fastener for the top; scrap of blue cotton and two 3" strips of ½"-wide decorative trim for the jeans.

Make a basic doll (page 17), adding hair and face as desired. Sleepover girl #1 is dressed in a blue-checked ribbon top and blue jeans.

1. To make the ribbon top, trim each short end of the checked ribbon at a 45° angle as shown. Fold a ¼"-wide hem to the wrong side of each angled edge,

and sew with tiny stitches. Stitch a tiny piece of Velcro fastener to the right side of one end and the wrong side of the other for fastening.

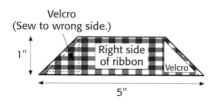

2. To make the jeans, trace the pants pattern (page 28) onto your preferred template material. Cut out the template. Follow the instructions for making the pirate, steps 2 through 5 (page 19), using the blue cotton to make the *full-length* pants. Do not hem the bottom edge of the pants. Instead, fray the raw edges to make fringe on both legs and stitch a 3" strip of ¼"-wide decorative trim to each leg, just above the fringe, for decoration. Do this before sewing the inseam.

Sleepover Girl #2 ("Sleepover Picnic")

You'll need: supplies for basic doll (page 17), scrap of red-flowered cotton and 7" strip of ½"-wide ribbon or trim for the dress, 10" length of ⅛"-wide red satin ribbon for belt (with additional, if desired, for pigtail ties), 4" length of 2"-wide ungathered eyelet for underpants.

Make a basic doll (page 17), adding hair and face as desired. Sleepover girl #2 is dressed in a red-flowered dress and tiny white eyelet underpants.

1. To make the dress, trace the dress pattern (page 28) onto your preferred template material. Cut out the template.

2. Fold a scrap of red-flowered cotton in half right sides together. Place the dress template on the fold of the fabric as shown, noting the grain line markings. Trace around the pattern with a sharp pencil and cut, adding a ¼"-wide seam allowance. Unfold the piece.

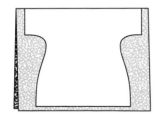

3. Cut a 2" x 2½" piece from the same red-flowered cotton for facing. Place the facing right sides together with the dress front, overlapping the short edge just slightly with the "shoulder fold" center as shown.

Use a pencil to trace the neckline (page 28) on the facing. Sew on the drawn line.

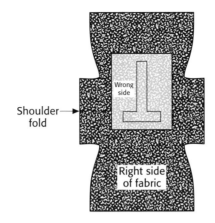

4. Use sharp embroidery scissors to slit an opening between the stitching completed in the previous step. Trim the seam allowances to a scant ¼" and clip the seams as necessary to make a neck opening. Turn the facing piece to the inside of the dress and press.

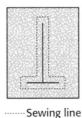

········ Sewing line
——— Cutting line

5. Hand sew tiny topstitches along the neck opening in matching thread. Hem each sleeve.

6. Sew the underarm and side seams; clip or notch all curves. Fold a ½"-wide strip of ribbon or lace trim over the bottom edge of the dress and stitch to finish.

7. Turn the garment right side out, dress the doll, and use the 10" length of ⅛"-wide red satin ribbon as a belt. If desired, use the

same satin ribbon to tie the doll's pigtails.

8. To make the underpants, follow the instructions for the little girl in the red dress, steps 5 through 7, on pages 20–21.

Sleepover Girl #3 ("Sleepover Picnic")

You'll need: supplies for basic doll (page 17), scrap of white-print cotton, 5" strip of ½"-wide ribbon or lace trim, and 1½" strip of ¼"-wide Velcro fastener for the blouse; 5" strip of ½"-wide ribbon or lace trim, 5" x 2" strip of red-print fabric (with selvage!), and tiny scrap of Velcro fastener for the skirt.

Make a basic doll (page 17), adding hair and face as desired. Sleepover girl #3 wears a white cotton blouse and red cotton skirt.

1. To make the blouse, trace the shirt/blouse front and back patterns (page 28) onto your preferred template material. Cut out the templates.

2. Fold a piece of white-print cotton right sides together. Place the shirt/blouse front template on the fabric, noting the grain-line markings. Trace around the

template with a sharp pencil and cut, adding a ¼"-wide seam allowance. You'll now have both the left and right blouse fronts.

3. Unfold the scrap and place the shirt/blouse back template on the fabric, once again noting the grain line. Trace around the template with a sharp pencil and cut, adding a ¼"-wide seam allowance.

4. Pin each front piece right sides together with the back piece, aligning the side seams. Sew both shoulder seams on the drawn line, and then sew a ¼"-wide hem on the sleeves and front edge of the blouse.

5. Sew both underarm and side seams. Clip or notch all curves and hem the bottom of the blouse.

6. Turn the garment right side out. Fold one 5" strip of ribbon or lace trim over the neckline and stitch to finish.

7. Stitch half of the 1½" Velcro-fastener strip to the right side of one front edge and the other half to the wrong side of the other front edge.

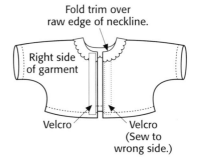

Fold trim over raw edge of neckline.

Right side of garment

Velcro   Velcro
          (Sew to
          wrong side.)

8. To make the skirt, fold the remaining 5" strip of ribbon or lace trim over the long raw (non-selvage) edge of the 5" x 2"

red-print fabric strip, and stitch to make a waistband. Stitch a ¼"-wide hem to the wrong side on both short raw edges.

9. Sew half of the tiny scrap of Velcro fastener to the wrong side of one corner of the waistband. Sew the other half of the Velcro fastener 1" from the opposite end of the waistband, this time on the right side. Dress the doll to finish.

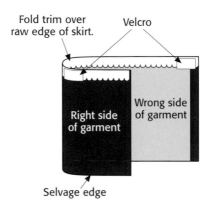

Fold trim over raw edge of skirt.   Velcro

Right side of garment   Wrong side of garment

Selvage edge

Sleepover Girl #4 ("Sleepover Picnic")

You'll need: supplies for basic doll (page 17), one 4½"-long piece of 2½"-wide gathered eyelet (or a 10" piece of ungathered eyelet gathered to 4½"), 13" length of ½"-wide ribbon or lace trim, and 4½" length of

⅛"-wide white satin ribbon for the dress; 4" length of 2"-wide ungathered eyelet for underpants.

Make a basic doll (page 17), adding hair and face as desired. Sleepover girl #4 wears a white eyelet dress and tiny matching underpants.

1. Hand or machine stitch a ¼"-wide hem on both short raw edges of the gathered eyelet.

2. Fold the 13" length of ribbon or lace trim lengthwise, wrong sides together, and press. Matching midpoints, fold the pressed ribbon over the gathered edge of the eyelet and stitch from one end of the ribbon to the other.

3. Sew one end of the ⅛"-wide white satin ribbon to the wrong side of the waistband, right along the edge of the dress, and the other end about 3½" further along the waistband. Match the center point of the waistband between the ribbon ends with the center point of the ribbon loop, and tack the ribbon to the backside of the waistband. Slip the satin ribbon over the doll's shoulder, and wrap the dress around her, finishing the waistband with a pretty bow.

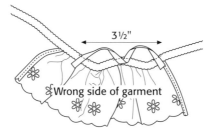

3½"

Wrong side of garment

4. To make the underpants, follow the instructions for the little girl in the red dress, steps 5 through 7, on pages 20–21.

Sleepover Girl #5 ("Sleepover Picnic")

You'll need: supplies for basic doll (page 17), black or navy solid cotton scrap and 2" strip of ¼"-wide Velcro fastener for the dress; 2½" x 3½" strip of white cotton fabric and 10" length of ¼"-wide white satin ribbon for the apron.

Make a basic doll (page 17), adding hair and face as desired. Sleepover girl #5 wears an Amish-style dress in a dark solid cotton with a white apron.

1. Make the dress with the robe/dress patterns on page 29 and follow the same instructions you used for making the train girl's robe (page 24). Use the dark solid scrap for the dress and omit the trim along the hemline. Finish the front with a strip of Velcro fastener just as you did for sleepover girl #3's blouse, step 7, on page 26.

2. To make the apron, sew a ¼"-wide hem on both long edges and 1 short edge of the white fabric strip. Fold over both corners on the unfinished short end and stitch in place; then hem the remaining short side.

3. Sew the 10" length of white satin ribbon about 1" from the top edge of the apron as shown, matching center points.

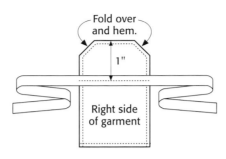

Fold over and hem.

1"

Right side of garment

4. Dress the doll and bind the hair in a ponytail or bun.

Sleepover Girl #6 ("Sleepover Picnic")

You'll need: supplies for basic doll (page 17), scrap of green print, 2½" length of green satin ribbon, and 1" strip of ¼"-wide Velcro fastener for the coveralls; 10" length of flowered trim for the belt.

Make a basic doll (page 17), adding hair and face as desired. The final sleepover girl (#6) is dressed in coveralls just like those worn by the pilot boy and girl (page 18).

Follow the instructions for making the coveralls on pages 18–19. Use the green print for the coveralls, finish the neckline with ribbon, and tie at the waist with the flowered trim.

Mini Doll ("Sleepover Picnic")

The sleepover girls are so lucky, they even have their own doll to play with! You'll need: supplies for basic doll (page 17), 4" piece of 1½"-wide embroidered eyelet (with large, ready-made holes along one finished edge) and 8" length of ⅜"-wide flowered ribbon or trim for the dress; 2¼" length of ½"-wide ungathered lace for the underpants.

Make a mini doll. Follow the instructions for the basic doll (body, hair, and face) on pages 17–18, but use the mini-doll pattern on page 28. The mini doll is dressed in an eyelet dress and tiny, lacy underpants.

1. For the dress, fold the eyelet right sides together, matching the short raw edges, and stitch.

2. Turn the garment right side out and thread the ribbon or trim through the ready-made holes, starting and ending at the seam.

3. Use the lace to make the underpants, following the instructions for the little girl in the red dress, steps 5–7, on pages 20–21.

4. Dress the doll; center the dress seam at the back and use loops in the ribbon for shoulder straps. Finish with a nice bow at the back seam.

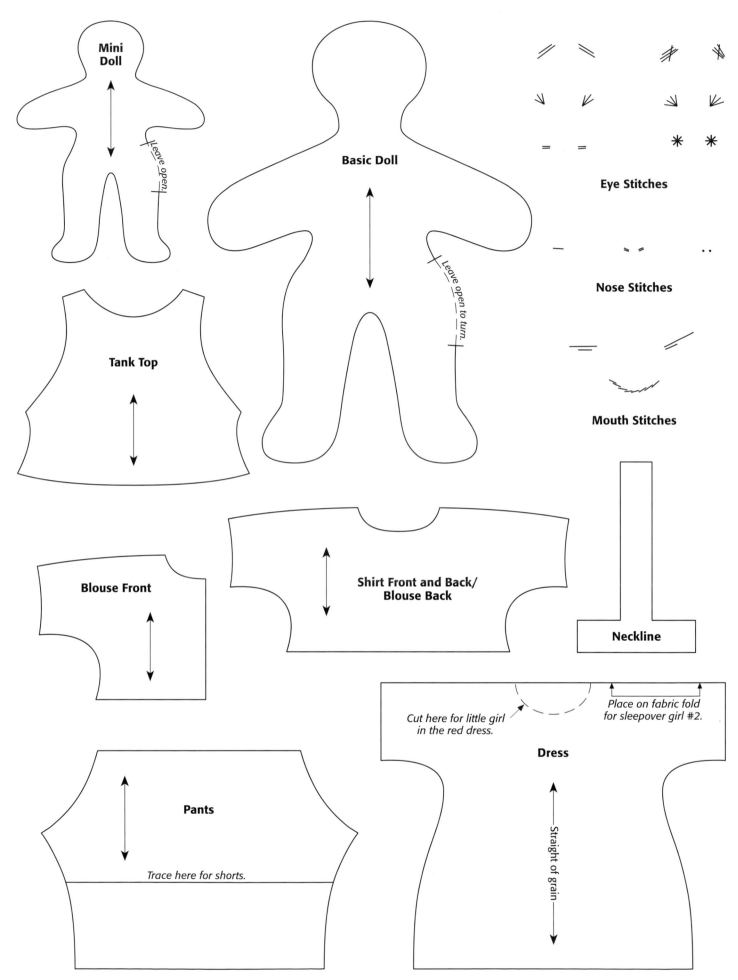

Mini Doll

Leave open.

Basic Doll

Leave open to turn.

Eye Stitches

Nose Stitches

Mouth Stitches

Tank Top

Blouse Front

Shirt Front and Back/
Blouse Back

Neckline

Cut here for little girl
in the red dress.

Place on fabric fold
for sleepover girl #2.

Dress

Straight of grain

Pants

Trace here for shorts.

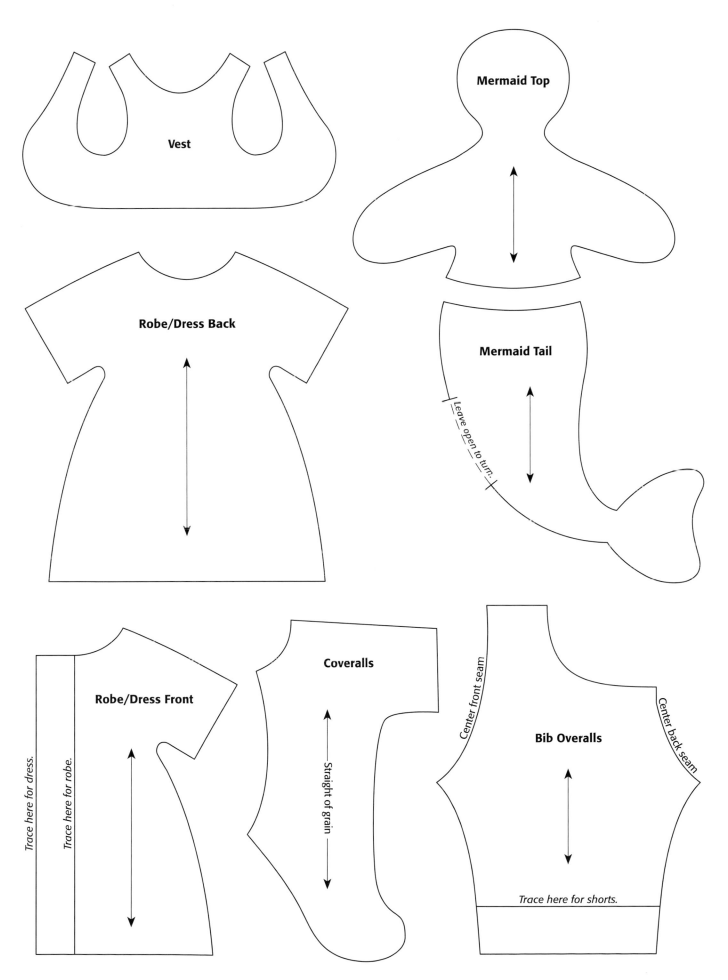

Vest

Mermaid Top

Robe/Dress Back

Mermaid Tail

Leave open to turn.

Robe/Dress Front

Trace here for dress.

Trace here for robe.

Coverals

Straight of grain

Center front seam

Center back seam

Bib Overalls

Trace here for shorts.

Two-Piece Animals

THE ANIMALS on the "Animal Train" quilt (page 89) are constructed in two separate pieces: body and head. To make the basic two-piece animal:

1. Trace the appropriate animal pattern (head and body) onto your preferred template material. Cut out the templates. Be sure to transfer the slit for turning.

2. Fold a piece of the desired fabric right sides together, and place each template on the fabric, noting the grain-line markings. Trace around each template with a sharp pencil, but *do not cut the fabric.*

3. Set your sewing machine for a very small stitch (e.g., 20 stitches per inch). Machine stitch around the entire shape, directly on the drawn line. Cut out the shape, adding a ¼"-wide seam allowance, and clip or notch all curves.

Note: *On smaller parts, such as ears, tails, and slender legs, you may need to trim to a ⅛"-wide seam allowance.*

4. Carefully cut a small slit in each piece as indicated by the transferred marking. Be sure to cut through 1 layer of fabric *only!* Turn each shape right side out.

5. Begin by stuffing the smallest areas first. Use batting scraps or stuffing and a knitting needle or dull pencil as needed. (Be careful not to poke any holes!) You don't need to stuff the tails; they are more lifelike when left unstuffed. Add additional stuffing to the shape until the entire piece is well filled. Whipstitch the slits closed.

6. Position the head on the body with the slits facing each other. Use thread in a matching color to sew the head to the body, catching the underside of the head so the stitches don't show.

7. Use glass seed beads and/or embroidery to add facial features as suggested. Refer to the patterns for guidance in placing these details.

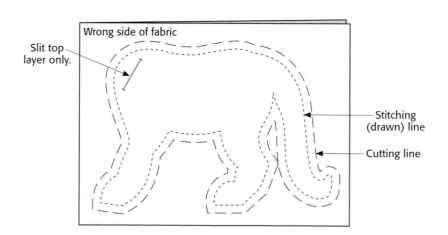

Wrong side of fabric

Slit top layer only.

Stitching (drawn) line

Cutting line

Elephant

You'll need: scraps of 2 different subtle gray prints, batting scraps or stuffing, 2 red seed beads.

Make the basic two-piece animal (left) using the elephant pattern pieces on pages 32–33 and the 2 gray-print scraps. Leave the tail unstuffed. Use the red seed beads for eyes.

Zebra

You'll need: scraps of black-and-white striped fabric, batting scraps or stuffing, 2 blue seed beads.

Make the basic two-piece animal (left) using the zebra pattern pieces on pages 31–32. Use the black-and-white striped scraps for both pieces, taking care with the direction of the stripes. Leave the tail unstuffed. How about blue seed-bead eyes?

Giraffe

You'll need: scraps of 2 different orange fabrics (one checked, one solid or subtle print), batting scraps or stuffing, 2 red seed beads.

Make the basic two-piece animal (page 30) using the giraffe pattern pieces on pages 32–33. Use the checked fabric scraps for the body and the solid or subtle print scraps for the head. Leave the neck open for turning; stitch closed before adding the head. Leave the tail unstuffed and add red seed-bead eyes.

Lion

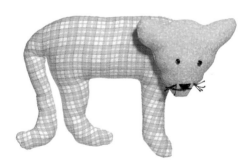

You'll need: scraps of 2 different yellow fabrics (1 plaid, 1 solid or subtle print), batting scraps or stuffing, 2 blue seed beads, black embroidery thread.

Make the basic two-piece animal (page 30) using the lion pattern pieces on pages 31–32. Use the plaid fabric scraps for the body and the subtle yellow scraps for the head. Leave the tail unstuffed. Add blue seed-bead eyes and use black embroidery thread to stitch a nose, mouth, and whiskers.

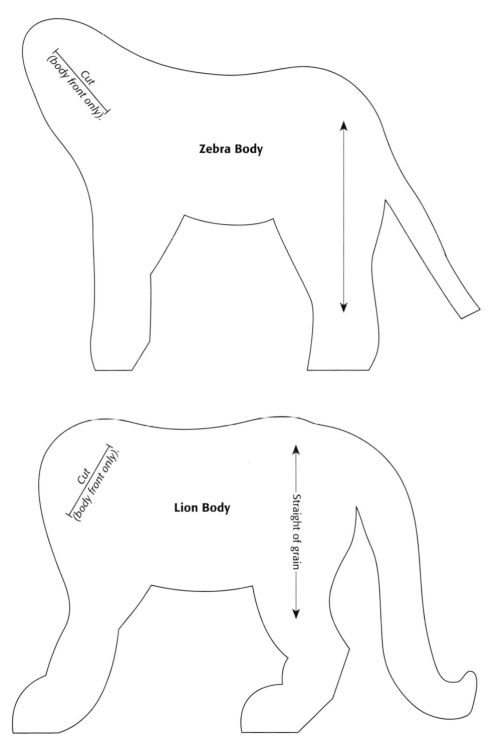

Cut (body front only).

Zebra Body

Cut (body front only).

Lion Body

Straight of grain

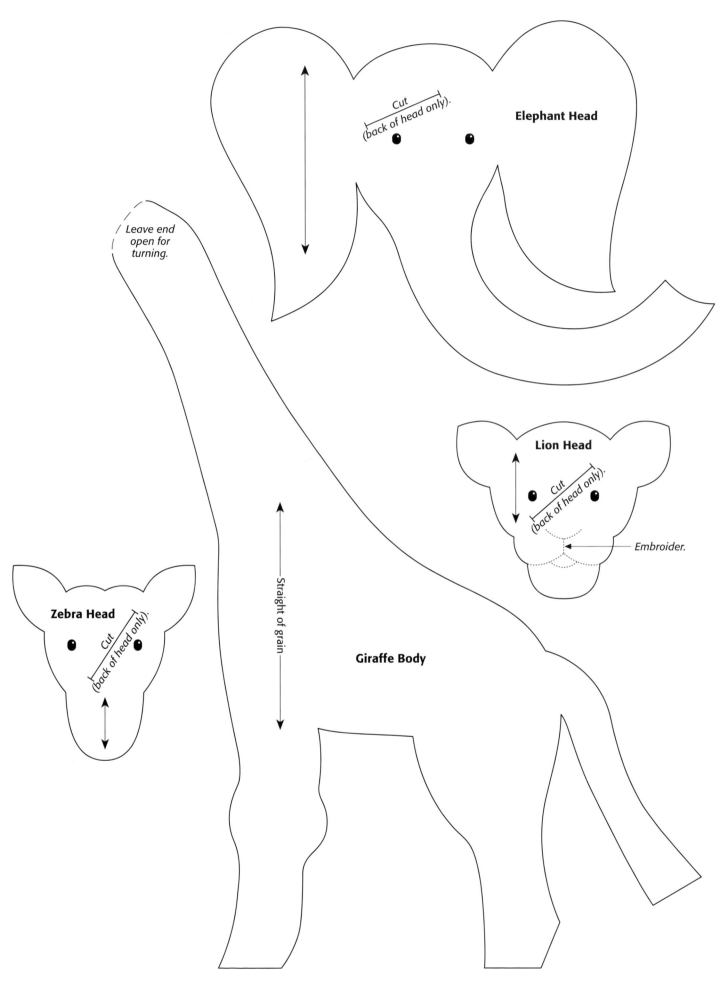

Cut (back of head only).

Elephant Head

Leave end open for turning.

Lion Head

Cut (back of head only).

Embroider.

Straight of grain

Zebra Head

Cut (back of head only).

Giraffe Body

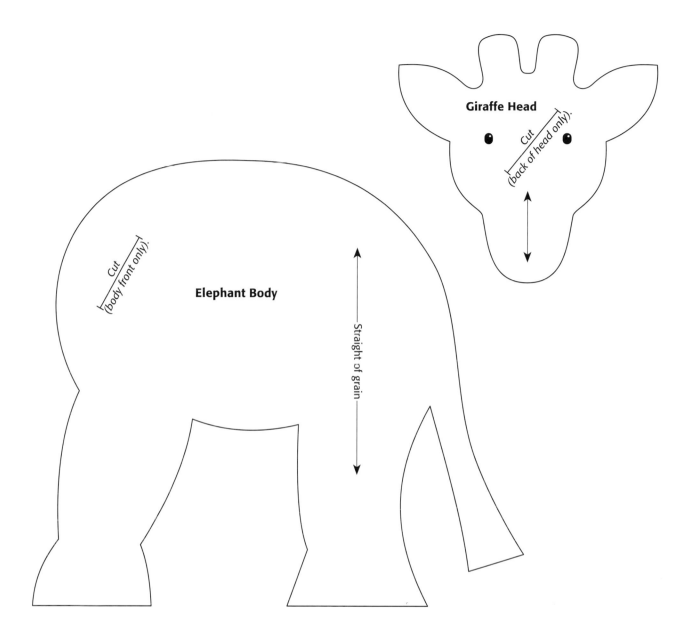

Giraffe Head

Cut
(back of head only).

Elephant Body

Cut
(body front only).

Straight of grain

One-Piece Animals

ALL REMAINING animal toys are constructed as a single piece, similar to the technique used to construct the basic doll (page 17).

To make the basic one-piece animal:

1. Trace the appropriate animal pattern onto your preferred template material. Cut out the template.

2. Fold a piece of the desired fabric right sides together, and place the template on the fabric noting the grain-line markings. Trace around the template with a sharp pencil, but *do not cut the fabric.*

3. Set your sewing machine for a very small stitch (e.g., 20 stitches per inch) or tiny zigzag. Machine stitch on the drawn line, leaving an opening as indicated on the pattern for turning. Sew a second time to reinforce for vigorous play. Cut out the figure, adding a ¼"-wide seam allowance. Clip or notch all curves.

4. Turn the figure right side out. Begin by stuffing the limbs and other small outer areas and "crannies" first, using batting scraps or stuffing and a knitting needle or dull pencil as needed. (Be careful not to poke any holes!) You don't need to stuff the tails. Add additional stuffing to the shape until the entire piece is well filled.

5. Close the opening with a blind or ladder stitch.

6. Use seed beads, embroidery, or permanent fabric pens to add features as suggested. Refer to the patterns for guidance in placing these details.

7. Some of these animals are buttoned to the quilt with loops made from matching ⅛"-wide satin ribbon. Measure the diameter of the button you will use, and multiply by 4. Cut the ribbon to this length; then align and stitch the short raw edges. Use matching thread to sew the ribbon loop to the back of the animal, turning under the short stitched edge.

> **Note:** *As an alternative for some of the smaller animals, you might use a small loop of narrow elastic or a small piece of looped trim instead of a ribbon loop.*

Mice ("Lunar Landing")

There is 1 each of mouse #1 and mouse #2 on the moon quilt. For each mouse, you'll need: scrap of gray solid or subtle-print fabric, batting scraps or stuffing, 2 red seed beads. Neither mouse has a hanging loop.

Make the basic one-piece animal (pages 33–34) using either mouse pattern #1 or #2 on page 41. Use a gray solid or print fabric scrap for each mouse. Leave most of the tail unstuffed, and add red seed-bead eyes to finish.

Fish ("Pirate Ship")

There are 5 fish on the pirate quilt. For each figure, you'll need: scrap of red, orange, or yellow solid or subtle-print fabric, batting scraps or stuffing, 2 seed beads, embroidery thread to match fabric for the fish; ⅛"-wide matching satin ribbon or narrow elastic for the hanging loop.

Make the basic one-piece animal (pages 33–34) for each fish using the fish pattern on page 39 and a red, orange, or yellow fabric scrap. Add seed-bead eyes and embroidered details, such as fins, to make the fish seem more lifelike.

Devil Ray ("Pirate Ship")

You'll need: scrap of subtle black-and-brown print, batting scraps or stuffing, 2 seed beads, 3" length of narrow (¼"- to ½"-wide) gold trim for the devil ray; narrow elastic for the hanging loop.

Make the basic one-piece animal (pages 33–34) using the devil ray pattern on page 40 and the black-and-brown-print scrap. Insert the narrow gold trim in the seam line to make a "tail" and add seed-bead eyes.

Seagull ("Pirate Ship")

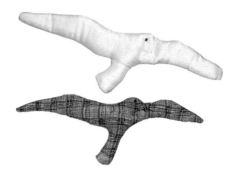

There are 3 seagulls on the pirate quilt. For each figure, you'll need: scrap of white or gray solid or subtle-print fabric, batting scraps or stuffing, 2 seed beads, embroidery thread to match fabric for the seagull; ⅛"-wide matching satin ribbon or narrow elastic for the hanging loop.

Make the basic one-piece animal (pages 33–34) for each seagull using the seagull pattern on page 40 and a white or gray fabric scrap. Seed-bead eyes and a few key embroidery stitches help define the head and beak.

Dolphin ("Pirate Ship")

You'll need: scrap of black solid or subtle-print fabric, batting scraps or stuffing, 2 gold seed beads, fine-point gold permanent fabric pen, embroidery thread to match fabric for the dolphin; ⅛"-wide matching satin ribbon or narrow elastic for the hanging loop.

Make the basic one-piece animal (pages 33–34) using the dolphin pattern on page 40 and the black fabric scrap. Add gold seed-bead eyes and use the gold permanent pen to define the "beak." Use embroidery thread to stitch a few key details.

Tiger Shark ("Pirate Ship")

You'll need: scrap of gray solid or subtle-print fabric, batting scraps or stuffing, 2 silver seed beads, and embroidery thread to match fabric for the shark; ⅛"-wide matching satin ribbon or narrow elastic for the hanging loop.

Make the basic one-piece animal (pages 33–34) using the tiger shark pattern on page 39 and the gray fabric scrap. Add silver seed-bead eyes, and use embroidery thread to stitch a few key details.

Octopus ("Pirate Ship")

Although this toy is technically constructed in 2 sections, you will make it using the instructions for the basic one-piece animal. You'll need: scraps of various red and orange solid or subtle-print fabrics, batting scraps, 2 large seed beads for the octopus; ⅛"-wide matching satin ribbon for the hanging loop.

1. Follow steps 1 through 4 in the instructions for the basic one-piece animal (pages 33–34) using the octopus pattern on page 40. Use a red solid or subtle-print scrap for the body and leave the end open as shown. Turn the piece right side out and stuff about half full with batting.

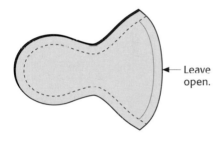

Leave open.

2. Use matching thread to run a gathering stitch all around the opening in the partially stuffed body, turning under the raw edge as you stitch. Set aside.

3. To make the tentacles, cut a total of eight 1½" x 10" strips from various red and orange fabric scraps. Fold each strip lengthwise, right sides together, and sew. Leave both short ends open.

4. Use a safety pin to turn each tentacle right side out. Cut eight 1" x 10" strips of batting. Roll each strip of batting lengthwise and use a safety pin to coax the rolled batting into the tentacles to stuff them. Hand stitch each tentacle closed at one end with matching thread.

5. Place the tentacles side by side as shown and join them by stitching over the unsewn edges. This stitching keeps the tentacles together and makes them easier to handle.

Stitch.

6. Insert the stitched end of the tentacles into the opening in the body, add additional batting, and tighten the gathering thread. Use matching thread to secure the tentacles with small hand stitches.

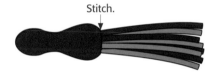
Stitch.

7. Add large seed-bead eyes and a ribbon loop as described in step 7, page 34.

Cow and Calf ("On the Farm")

Both a cow and her calf appear on the farm quilt. For each figure, you'll need: scrap of black or brown solid or subtle-print fabric, batting scraps or stuffing, 1 or 2 seed beads,

6" length of ⅛"-wide red satin ribbon, and a tiny "gold" cowbell. For the calf, you'll also need black or brown yarn scraps for the tail. Neither figure has a hanging loop.

For each figure, make the basic one-piece animal (pages 33–34) using either the cow or calf pattern on page 42. Use a black or brown fabric scrap for each animal and leave the tail unstuffed. Add a tassel made from matching-colored yarn to the end of the calf's tail. Finish with seed-bead eyes, a red ribbon necktie, and tiny cowbell.

> ## Tip
>
> **Secure the cowbell to the ribbon with a secure knot—for safety's sake! Do not give any of the quilts in this book to children younger than three.**

Pigs and Piglets ("On the Farm")

There are 4 pigs—2 adults and 2 babies—on the farm quilt. For each figure, you'll need: scrap of pink solid, checked, or subtle-print fabric, batting scraps or stuffing, 1 or 2 seed beads. None of the pigs has a hanging loop.

For each member of the pig family, make the basic one-piece animal (pages 33–34) using the pattern for pig #1, pig #2, or the piglet on pages 42–43. Use a pink fabric scrap for each, and add seed-bead eyes to finish.

Horse
("On the Farm")

Your horse may be a palomino, a pinto, a roan, or any color you wish, depending upon the fabric you choose. You'll need: fabric scrap in your preferred color and/or print, batting scraps or stuffing, matching yarn scraps, 2 seed beads, 8" length of ⅛"-wide satin ribbon. The horse does not have a hanging loop.

Make the basic one-piece animal (pages 33–34) using the horse pattern on page 43. Insert a matching colored tassel "tail" before sewing the seam line. Tack a matching fringed "mane" to the horse's head after the figure is turned and stuffed. Finish with seed-bead eyes and a narrow blue ribbon "rein."

Cat
("On the Farm")

You'll need: scrap of solid or print fabric in preferred "cat" color, batting scraps or stuffing, 2 seed beads, black embroidery thread. The cat does not have a hanging loop.

Make the basic one-piece animal (pages 33–34) using the cat pattern on page 43 and your chosen fabric scrap. Yellow-green seed beads are perfect for cat eyes. Use the black thread to embroider whiskers.

Hen
("On the Farm")

There are 3 hens on the farm quilt. For each hen, you'll need: scrap of white-solid or subtle-print fabric, scraps of red-solid and orange-solid fabric, batting scraps or stuffing, 4½" length of yellow yarn, tiny scraps of iron-on fusible web, 2 seed beads for the hen; ⅛"-wide red satin ribbon for the hanging loop.

1. For each hen body, cut 1 square, 1¼" x 1¼", and 1 square, 2⅛" x 2⅛", from the white fabric scrap. Divide the larger square along 1 diagonal to make 2 triangles.

2. From the red scrap, cut 3 squares, each 1" x 1", for the comb and the feet. From the orange scrap, cut 1 square, 1" x 1", for the beak.

3. Fold one 1" red square (comb) and the 1" orange square in half, and then fold each again as shown.

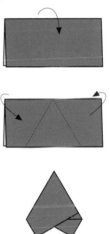

4. Place the white triangles right sides together, and sew the 2 shorter sides. Stitch the folded beak and comb in the seam, between the layers, pointing inward as shown.

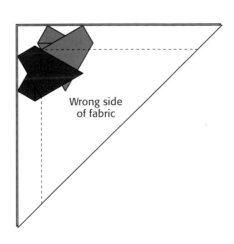

Wrong side of fabric

5. Use matching thread to hand stitch the remaining (1½") white square to the open edge of the triangle unit from step 4. Match opposite corners of the square with each seam. Match the remaining 2 corners with the center point of each long, diagonal edge. Leave a small opening for turning.

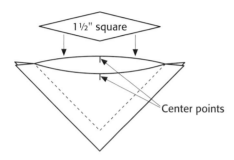

1½" square

Center points

Leave open.

6. Turn the figure right side out, stuff tightly, and close by hand with a ladder or blind stitch.

7. To make the legs, knot one end of the length of yellow yarn. Use iron-on fusible web to layer the remaining two 1" red squares wrong sides together. Cut the square on both diagonals to make 4 small triangles.

8. Thread a large needle with the knotted yellow yarn. Thread 2 red triangle "feet" on the yellow yarn leg. Make another knot about 1" away for a knee; make another about 1" beyond that. Stitch the yarn through the hen and knot on the other side. Make a knot for the other knee,

thread on the remaining 2 triangle feet, and finish with a knot.

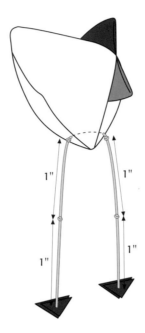

1"   1"

1"   1"

9. Add seed-bead eyes and finish with a red ribbon loop at the hen's tail for hanging (see step 7, page 34).

Teddy Bear ("Sleepover Picnic")

You'll need: scrap of checked cotton fabric (approximately 7" x 16"), batting scraps or stuffing, 3 tiny black buttons, 8" length of

¼"-wide satin ribbon. The teddy bear does not have a hanging loop.

1. Trace the teddy bear pattern (page 44) onto your preferred template material. Cut out the template.

2. Fold the checked cotton fabric right sides together. Place the bear template on the fabric, taking careful note of the grain-line markings. Trace around the template with a sharp pencil and cut, adding a ¼"-wide seam allowance. Trace and cut 2 units. Each unit yields both a regular and a reverse piece.

3. To make the bear front, pin a regular and a reverse piece right sides together and sew the center seam from dot to dot as shown on the pattern. Repeat to sew the bear back.

4. Place the bear front and the back right sides together, making sure to align the center seams. Sew around the bear, leaving an opening to turn as indicated on the pattern. Clip or notch all curves.

5. Turn the figure right side out and stuff and stitch as described for the basic one-piece animal, steps 4 and 5 (page 34). Finish with securely stitched black button eyes and nose and a narrow ribbon necktie.

Rabbit
("Sleepover Picnic")

You'll need: scrap of white-solid or subtle-print fabric, batting scraps or stuffing, 2 blue seed beads, 1 slightly larger pink bead, white embroidery thread for the rabbit; ⅛"-wide piece of white satin ribbon for the hanging loop.

Make the basic one-piece animal (pages 33–34) using the rabbit pattern on page 44 and the white fabric scrap. Use the blue seed beads for eyes and the slightly larger pink bead for the nose. Add embroidery stitches to better define the individual ears.

Dragon
("Sleepover Picnic")

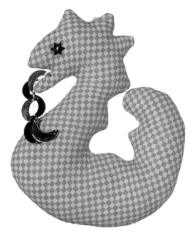

You'll need: scrap of yellow-and-orange-checked fabric, batting scraps or stuffing, 2 tiny star sequins, 2 tiny blue seed beads, string of colorful sequins or spangles for the dragon; ⅛"-wide matching satin ribbon for the hanging loop.

Make the basic one-piece animal (pages 33–34) using the dragon pattern on page 44 and the checked fabric scrap. Use the tiny blue seed beads to secure star-sequin eyes, and add a string of colorful spangles at the dragon's mouth for "fire."

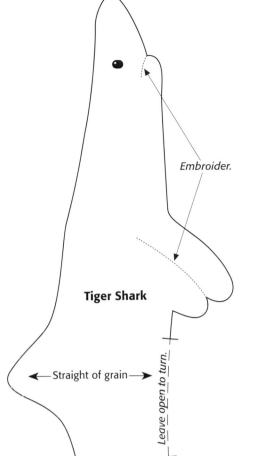

Embroider.

Tiger Shark

← Straight of grain →

Leave open to turn.

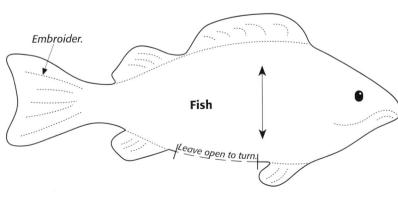

Embroider.

Fish

Leave open to turn.

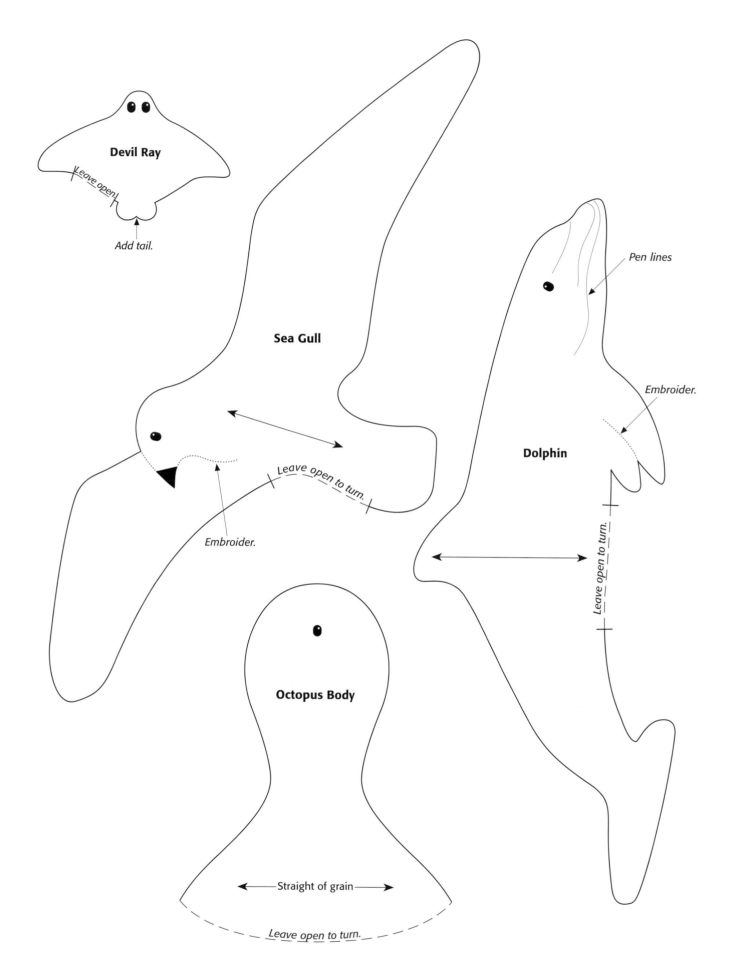

Devil Ray

Leave open!

Add tail.

Sea Gull

Embroider.

Leave open to turn.

Embroider.

Octopus Body

Straight of grain

Leave open to turn.

Dolphin

Pen lines

Embroider.

Leave open to turn.

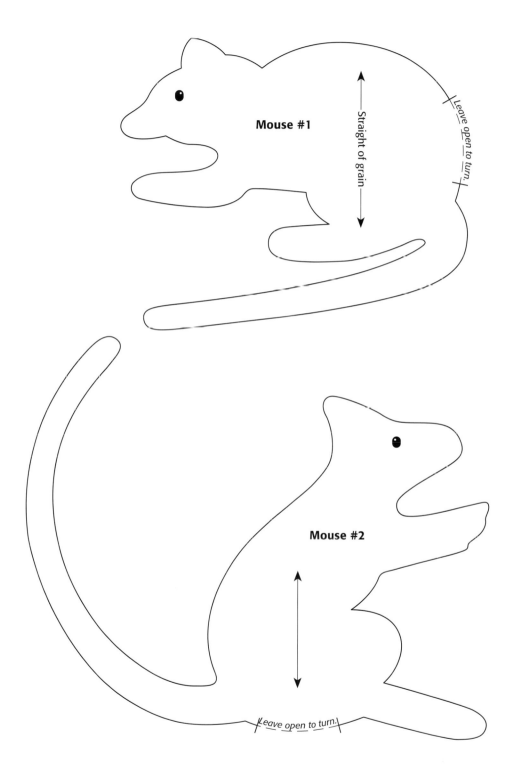

Mouse #1

Straight of grain

Leave open to turn.

Mouse #2

Leave open to turn.

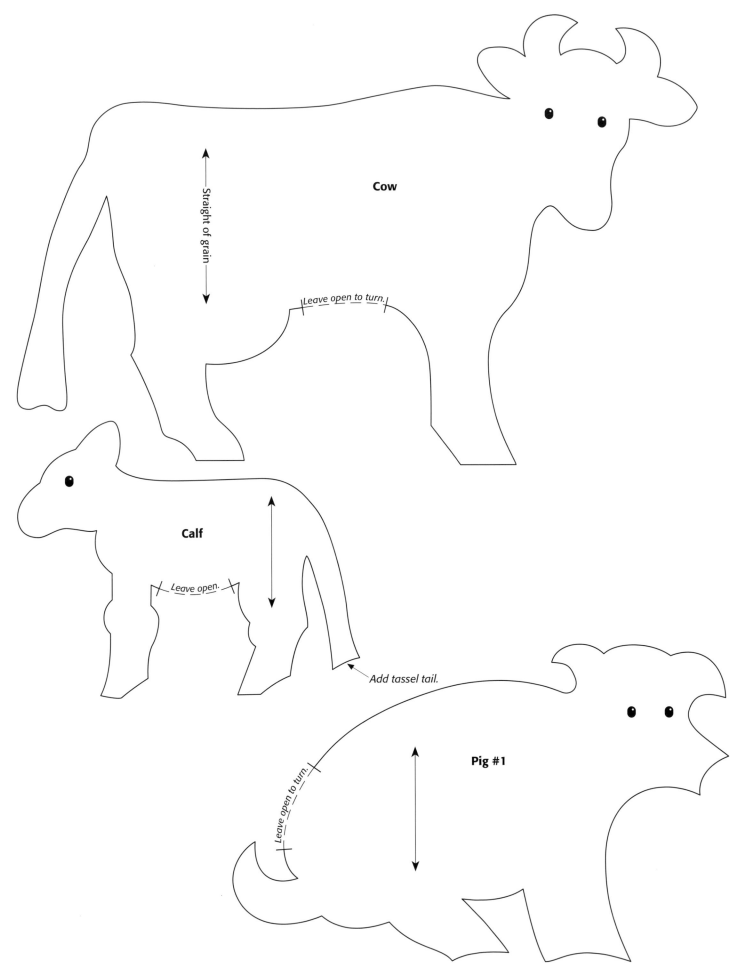

Cow

Straight of grain

Leave open to turn.

Calf

Leave open.

Add tassel tail.

Leave open to turn.

Pig #1

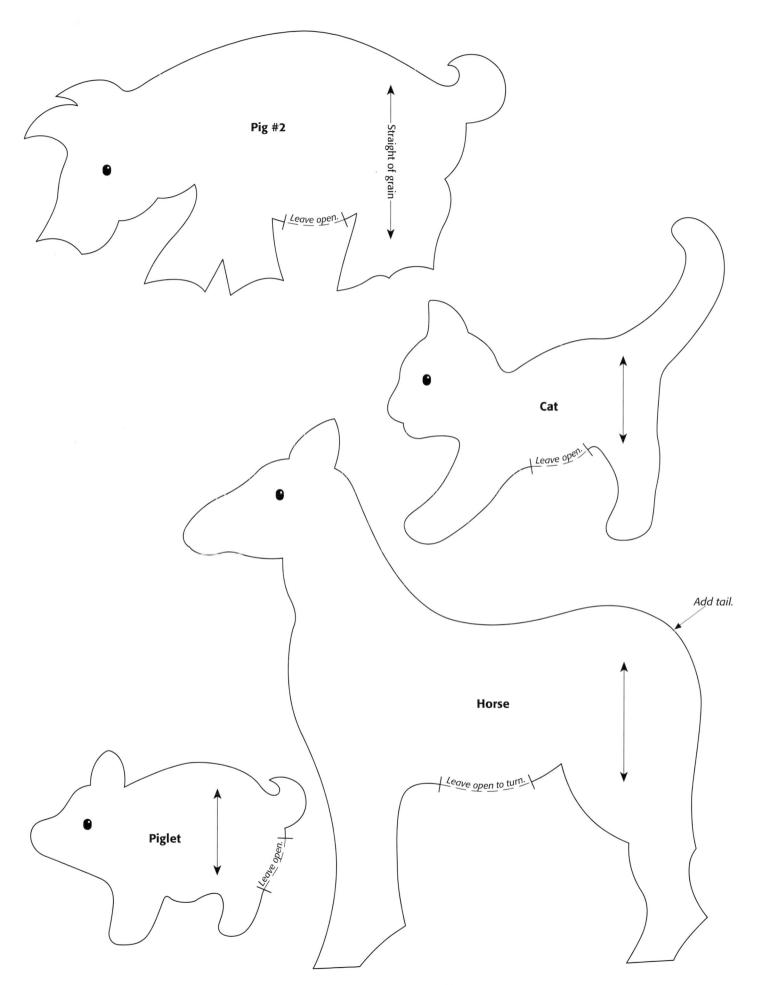

Pig #2

Straight of grain

Leave open.

Cat

Leave open.

Add tail.

Horse

Leave open to turn.

Piglet

Leave open.

Leave open.

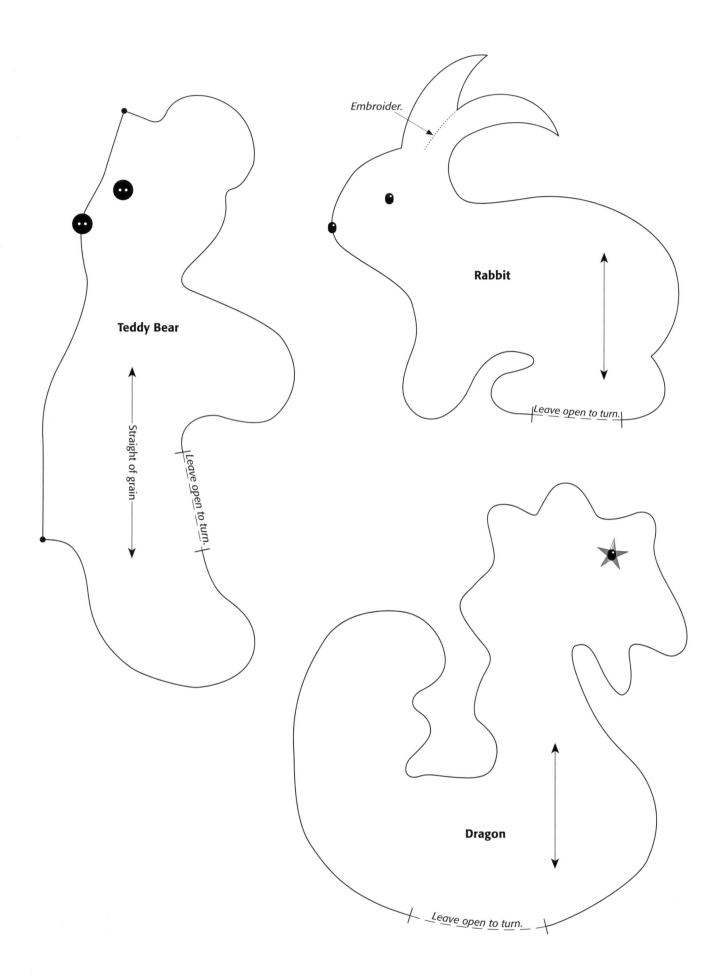

Embroider.

Rabbit

Teddy Bear

Straight of grain

Leave open to turn.

Leave open to turn.

Dragon

Leave open to turn.

Moveable Flat Toys

THERE ARE many theme-related flat items attached to the quilts with buttons. Children can reposition them around the quilt at will. To make the basic moveable flat toy:

1. Trace the appropriate pattern onto your preferred template material. Cut out the template.

2. Fold a piece of the desired fabric (or layer 2 different fabrics) right sides together, and center the layers over a slightly larger piece of batting. Place the template on the top layer of fabric, noting the grain-line markings. Trace around the template with a sharp pencil, but *do not cut the fabric*.

3. Set your sewing machine for a very small stitch (e.g., 20 stitches per inch) or tiny zigzag. Machine stitch on the drawn line, leaving an opening as indicated on the pattern. Cut out the figure, adding a ¼"-wide seam allowance. Clip or notch all curves.

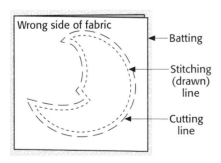

4. Turn the figure right side out, so the layer of batting is between the 2 fabric layers, and press.

5. Close the opening with a blind or ladder stitch, turning the seam allowance to the inside as you sew.

6. Add lines of quilting or other stitching for detail if desired.

7. Select a button (or buttons) to attach the toy to the quilt. Measure the button and refer to your sewing machine manual to make a buttonhole to fit. Position the buttonhole as indicated on the pattern.

Button-On Sun ("Lunar Landing")

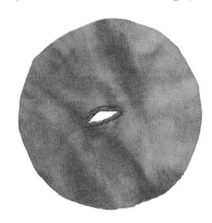

You'll need: scrap of mottled yellow-orange print for sun front, scrap of black solid fabric for sun backing, batting scrap.

Make the basic moveable flat toy (left) using the Saturn/button-on-sun pattern on page 50.

Planet Earth ("Lunar Landing")

You'll need: scraps of blue "stripey" print for Earth front and backing, batting scrap.

Make the basic moveable flat toy (left) using the Earth/Uranus (outer) pattern on page 50.

> **Note:** *This same pattern is adapted to make the half-suns stitched to the binding on "Lunar Landing" (page 56). See the specific quilt instructions for details.*

Uranus ("Lunar Landing")

Uranus is constructed in 2 separate units (planet and ring) that are stitched together in the final step. You'll need: scraps of 2 different blue subtle-print fabrics for the planet and ring fronts, scrap of black solid fabric for planet and ring backings; batting scraps.

1. For each of the 2 units (planet and ring), make the basic moveable flat toy (page 45). Use the Earth/Uranus (outer) pattern on page 50 for Uranus, and the ring #2 pattern on page 51 for the ring. Make a buttonhole in the planet only (not the ring!).

2. Refer to the photo on page 45. Slip the ring over the planet and secure it to the back of the figure with a blind stitch in matching-colored thread.

Saturn ("Lunar Landing")

Saturn is constructed in 3 separate units (planet and rings) that are stitched together in the final step. You'll need: scraps of 3 different brightly-colored print fabrics for the planet and ring fronts, scraps of unbleached muslin for planet and ring backings, batting scraps.

1. For each of the 3 units (planet and each ring), make the basic moveable flat toy (page 45). Use the Saturn/button-on sun pattern on page 50 for the planet and the ring #1 and #2 patterns on page 51 for the rings. Make a buttonhole in the planet only (not the rings!).

2. Refer to the photo at left. Place the smaller ring (#1) inside the larger one (#2) and sew a few tacking stitches on each end with matching thread to hold the rings together.

3. Slip the ring set over the planet and secure it to the back of the figure with a blind stitch in matching thread.

Spaceship ("Lunar Landing")

The spaceship is constructed in 2 units: A (upper) and B (lower). The units are buttoned together before being attached to the quilt. To make the entire spaceship, you'll need: large scrap of shiny, silver fabric for spaceship front, ½ yd. black solid fabric for spaceship linings and backings, thin batting scraps, 1 gray or silver button.

To make each unit of the spaceship:

1. Trace the appropriate spaceship pattern (A, page 51, or B, page 52) onto your preferred template material. Cut out the template.

2. You'll need to cut 4 fabric pieces for each unit. Place the template on the back side of the shiny, silver fabric, noting the grain-line markings. Trace around the

outside edge of the pattern (not the center opening!) with a sharp pencil. Cut out the piece, adding a ¼"-wide seam allowance. *Do not cut out the center opening!* Repeat to trace and cut 3 identical pieces from the black fabric and 1 identical piece from the batting.

3. Pin the silver piece and 1 black piece right sides together. Place the template over the black fabric, and trace the center opening onto the fabric. Remove the template and sew directly on the line, all around the center opening. Carefully cut away the opening, cutting through both layers and leaving a ¼"-wide seam allowance. Trim and clip and/or notch all seam allowances and corners as needed to reduce bulk. Turn the piece right side out and press.

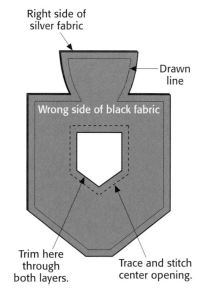

Right side of silver fabric

Drawn line

Wrong side of black fabric

Trim here through both layers.

Trace and stitch center opening.

4. Layer the unit from step 3 (silver side up), 1 remaining black piece (wrong side up), the batting, and the final black piece (right side up). Pin the layers, and sew on the drawn line around the outside edge of the unit. Leave a small opening for turning as indicated on the pattern.

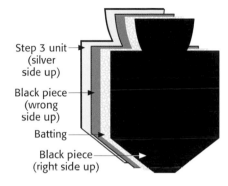

Step 3 unit (silver side up)

Black piece (wrong side up)

Batting

Black piece (right side up)

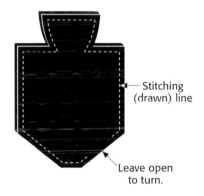

← Stitching (drawn) line

← Leave open to turn.

5. Clip and/or notch all seam allowances and corners as needed to reduce bulk. Turn the piece right side out so that the silver fabric is on top; press.

6. Make buttonholes in unit A, and sew the button to unit B as indicated on the pattern pieces. Refer to the photo on page 46, and button the lower unit to the upper unit to finish.

UFO ("Lunar Landing")

You'll need: scrap of dark red silk for UFO front, scrap of black solid fabric for UFO backing, batting scrap, 6 large and 6 small buttons.

Make the basic moveable flat toy (page 45) using the UFO pattern on page 53. I added a line of quilting to help define the UFO shape. Refer to the pattern for guidance in placing these details and the buttons.

Rowboat ("Pirate Ship")

The rowboat is constructed in 2 halves that are hand stitched together to finish the toy. For the entire boat, you'll need: scraps of dark brown subtle print for the outside of the boat, black solid fabric for the boat lining, batting scraps.

1. Follow the instructions for the basic moveable flat toy, steps 1 through 6 (page 45) to make each half of the boat. Use the boat pattern on page 54, the dark brown print for the front,

and the black solid for the lining (backing) of each half. Hand or machine quilt each half of the boat as indicated on the pattern for added detail.

2. Make a buttonhole in one half of the boat as indicated on the pattern piece.

3. Pin the 2 halves of the boat right sides together and use matching thread to whipstitch them along the bottom, curved edge. Turn the boat right side out, and repeat on the outside bottom edge.

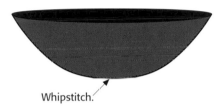

Whipstitch.

Scarecrow ("On the Farm")

You'll need: scraps of black and yellow felt for the scarecrow, scrap of red-print fabric for hatband, tiny scraps of iron-on fusible web and various color fabrics for patches, ⅛"-wide black satin ribbon for hanging loop.

1. Trace the scarecrow patterns (page 54) onto your preferred template material. Cut out the templates.

2. Trace 2 of the hat onto a scrap of black felt and 2 of the shirt onto a scrap of yellow felt. Cut out each piece on the traced line.

3. Layer the hat pieces and use black thread to sew a zigzag stitch as indicated on the pattern piece. Repeat for the shoulders on the shirt.

4. Layer 2 remaining black felt scraps. Place the trouser template on the felt and trace. Cut on the drawn line.

5. Sew the center front and back seams with a ¼"-wide seam allowance as indicated on the pattern pieces.

6. Fold the trouser unit so the front and back seams are centered over each other. Sew the crotch seam with a ¼"-wide seam allowance. Clip and/or notch the seam allowance, trim the trouser legs with pinking shears, and turn the trousers right side out.

7. Tuck the shirt into the hat and the pants into the shirt. Use the black thread to attach the pieces with a zigzag stitch. Add details such as a hatband and iron-on scrappy patches as shown. Refer to the photo on page 47 and the pattern piece for guidance as needed.

8. Finish with a satin-ribbon loop as described for the basic one-piece animal, step 7, on page 34.

Sun ("Animal Train")

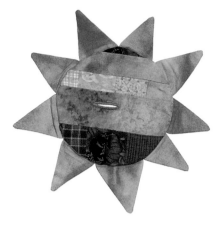

You'll need: scraps of yellow-orange print for front and backing of the rays, scraps of 5 or 6 yellow and orange prints for the strip-pieced sun front; scrap of yellow solid for sun backing, batting scraps.

1. Trace the sun and ray patterns (page 55) onto template material. Cut out the template.

2. Use the template to trace and cut a total of 18 ray pieces from the yellow-orange scraps, adding a ¼"-wide seam allowance to each piece. Place rays right sides together in pairs and sew the 2 sides as indicated on the pattern. Trim the tip and turn each ray right side out.

Note: *Instead of pivoting, stitch 1 or 2 stitches across top of ray to get a sharper point when turning.*

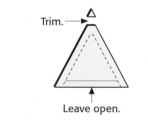

Trim. ➞

Leave open.

3. Sew the yellow- and orange-print scraps together to make a strip set measuring approximately 6" x 6". Press the seams to one side.

4. Trace the sun template onto the strip-pieced square and cut, adding a ¼"-wide seam allowance. Repeat to trace and cut the same shape from the yellow solid fabric for backing and also from the batting.

5. Place the batting on your work surface. Layer the yellow solid backing piece over it (right side up). Space and pin the rays around the perimeter of the sun with the sewn tips pointing inward. Center the strip-pieced sun on top of sandwich (wrong side up) and pin.

6. Sew around the perimeter of the circle on the drawn line, leaving a small opening for turning as indicated on the pattern. Clip or notch the curves as needed.

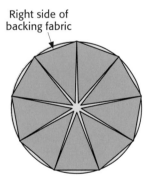

Right side of backing fabric

Arrange sun rays.

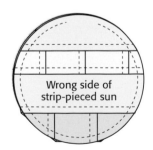

Wrong side of strip-pieced sun

Place strip-pieced sun wrong side down and stitch.

7. Turn the sun right side out and press carefully. Close the opening by hand with a blind or ladder stitch, and finish with a buttonhole as directed for the basic moveable flat toy, step 7 (page 45).

Moon ("Animal Train")

You'll need: scraps of 4 or 5 different red, yellow, and orange prints for the strip-pieced moon front; scrap of yellow solid fabric for moon backing; batting scrap.

1. Sew the red-, yellow-, and orange-print scraps together to make a strip set measuring approximately 7" x 7". Press the seams to one side.

2. Make the basic moveable flat toy (page 45) using the moon pattern on page 55 and the strip-pieced fabric for the moon front. When you attach the toy to the quilt, the button becomes the eye of the moon!

Moon ("Sleepover Picnic")

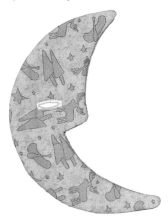

You'll need: scrap of yellow print for front, scrap of solid yellow for backing, batting scrap.

Make the basic moveable flat toy (page 45) using the moon pattern on page 55.

Campfire ("Sleepover Picnic")

You'll need: scraps of yellow, red, and orange fabrics; batting scraps or stuffing; 1 small snap fastener.

1. Trace the flame and base templates (page 54) onto your preferred template material. Cut out the templates.

2. Use the flame template to trace and cut a total of 18 flame pieces from the various yellow, red, and orange scraps, adding a ¼"-wide seam allowance to each piece. Place flames right sides together in pairs, and sew the 2 curved sides on the drawn lines. Leave the straight edge open for turning. Trim the tip, and turn each flame right side out. (See note on page 48.)

3. Place the flames side by side as shown, and join them by stitching over the unsewn edges.

Right side of fabric

4. Use the base template to trace and cut a campfire base from a scrap of red fabric, adding a ¼"-wide seam allowance. Use matching thread to baste around the perimeter of the circle, approximately ⅜" from the raw edge. Gather the circle right side out to form a small "bag."

5. Shape the straight-stitched edges of the flame unit into a circle and insert the flame unit, raw seam allowance first, into the bag. Vary the amount of flame inserted so flames vary in height. Pull the basting thread snug and knot it, turning the raw edge of the bag to the inside. For added security, use matching-colored thread to stitch the bag to the flames.

6. Sew one half of the snap fastener to the underside of the completed campfire unit. Stitch the other half to the quilt later to secure the campfire.

Snap

Saturn/Button-On Sun

Leave open to turn.

Buttonhole

Border Sun
Trace inner line.

Earth/Uranus
Trace outer line.

Leave open to turn.

Leave open to turn.

Buttonhole

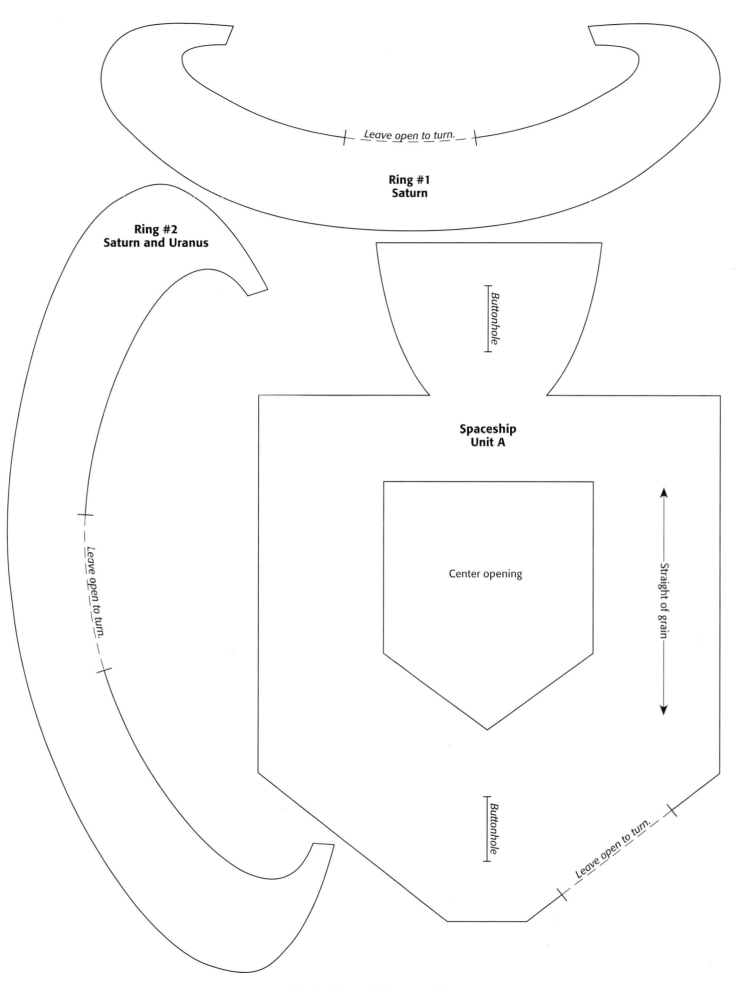

Ring #1
Saturn

Ring #2
Saturn and Uranus

Leave open to turn.

Leave open to turn.

Buttonhole

Spaceship
Unit A

Center opening

Straight of grain

Buttonhole

Leave open to turn.

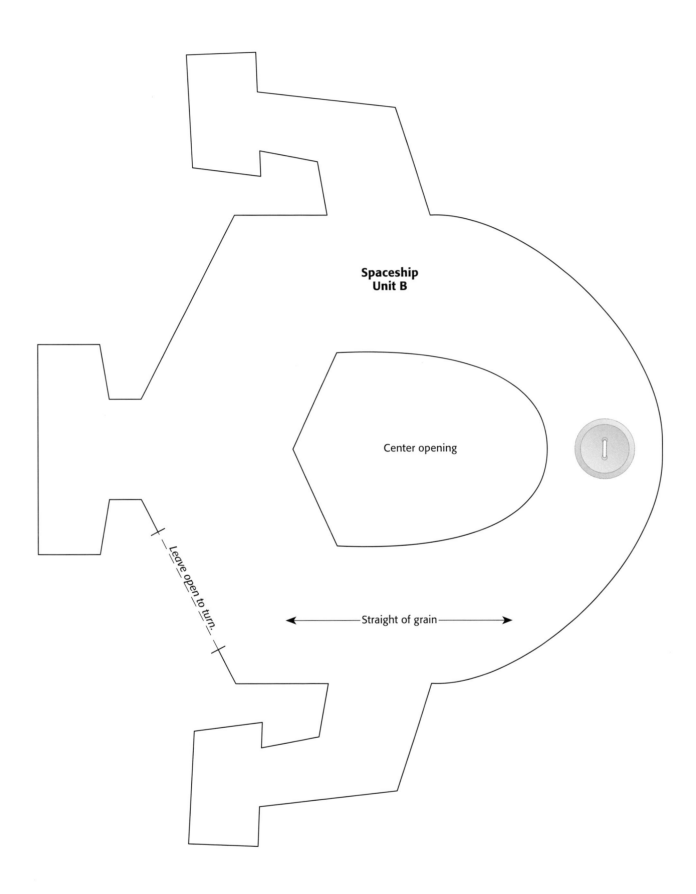

**Spaceship
Unit B**

Center opening

Leave open to turn.

←————— Straight of grain —————→

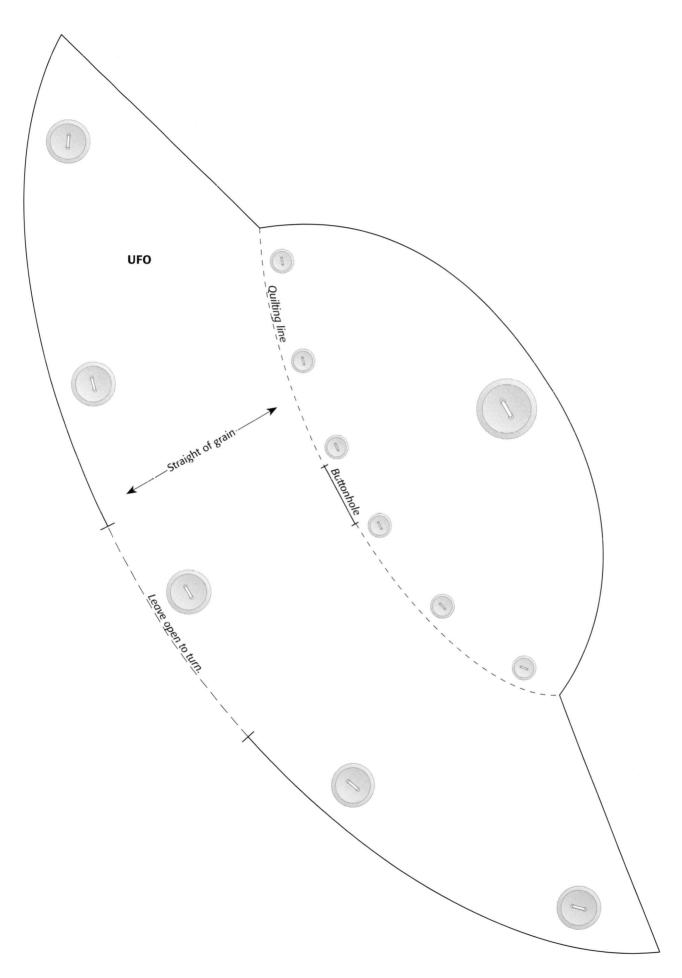

UFO

Quilting line

Straight of grain

Buttonhole

Leave open to turn.

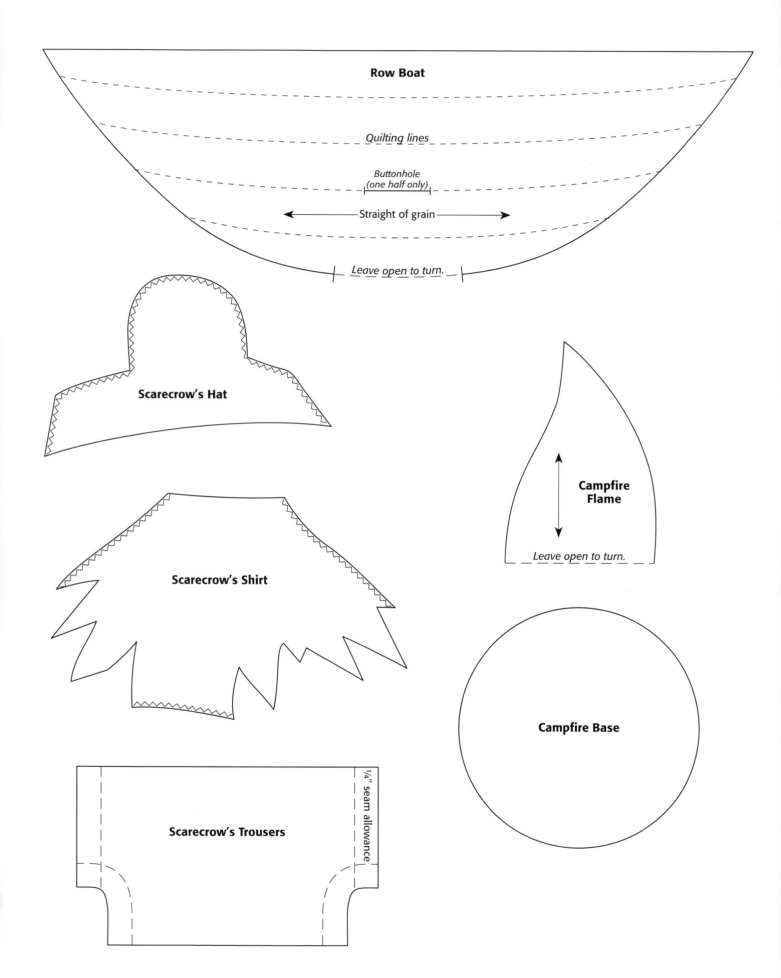

Row Boat

Quilting lines

Buttonhole
(one half only)

Straight of grain

Leave open to turn.

Scarecrow's Hat

Campfire
Flame

Leave open to turn.

Scarecrow's Shirt

Campfire Base

Scarecrow's Trousers

¼" seam allowance

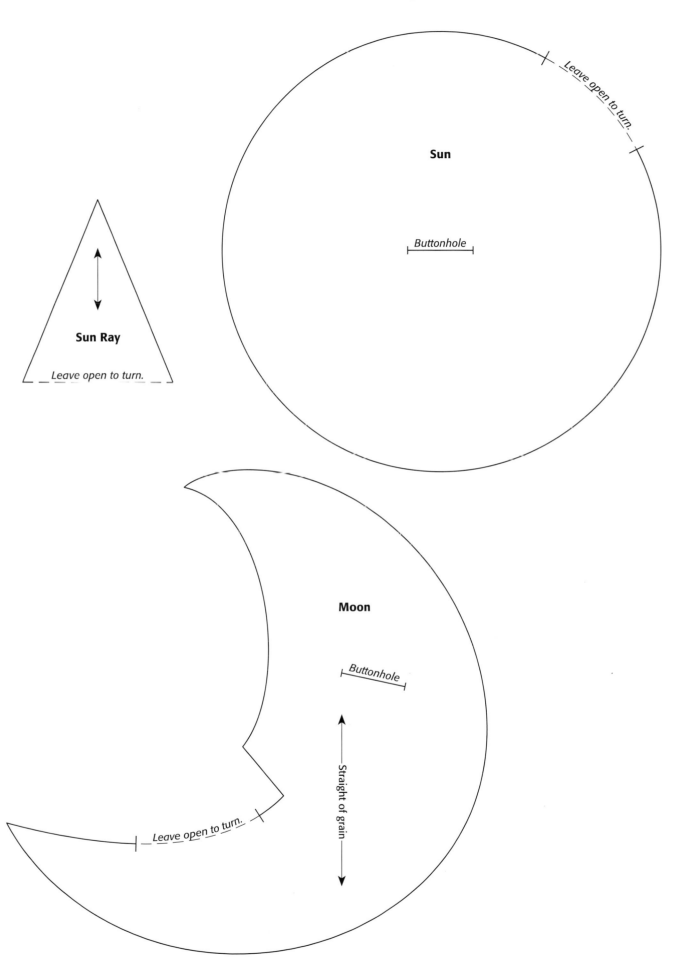

Sun

Buttonhole

Leave open to turn.

Sun Ray

Leave open to turn.

Moon

Buttonhole

Straight of grain

Leave open to turn.

Lunar Landing

Lunar Landing by Kristin Kolstad Addison, 2000, Førde, Norway.

Finished quilt size: 45" x 35"

Dolls: girl and boy pilot, 2 moon people

One-Piece Animals: 2 mice

Moveable Flat Toys: button-on sun, planet Earth, Uranus, Saturn, spaceship, UFO

Materials

42"-wide fabric

- ⅞ yd. black star print for background
- 1¼ yds. *total* of assorted yellow and orange prints for moon and moon-and-half-sun trim
- ¾ yd. yellow solid for moon facings and sun, moon, and moon-and-half-sun trim backings
- White and pink scraps for cow appliqué
- ¼ yd. white tone-on-tone print for inner borders
- ¼ yd. gray subtle print for middle borders
- ½ yd. black subtle print for outer borders
- ½ yd. yellow-orange mottled print for binding and sun rays
- 1½ yds. fabric for backing
- Fabric scraps and assorted notions for dolls, animals, and moveable flat toys*
- 50" x 40" piece of batting
- Yardstick compass (optional)
- Compass
- Freezer paper
- Fine-point black permanent marker
- Batting scraps for moon-and-half-sun trim
- 8 buttons for hanging assorted flat toys

* See instructions for specific doll, animal, or toy for fabrics and notions required.

Cutting

All measurements include ¼"-wide seam allowances.

From the black star print, cut:
- One piece, 37" x 27", for background

From the assorted yellow and orange prints, cut a *total* of:
- 4 strips, each 1" x 42", for large moon and moon-and-half-sun trim
- 4 strips, each 1½" x 42", for large moon and moon-and-half-sun trim
- 4 strips, each 2" x 42", for large moon and moon-and-half-sun trim
- 4 strips, each 2½" x 42", for large moon and moon-and-half-sun trim
- 4 strips, each 3" x 42", for large moon and moon-and-half-sun trim

From the yellow solid, cut:
- 4 squares, each 6" x 6", for moon facing

From the white tone-on-tone print, cut:
- 4 strips, each 1" x 42", for inner borders

From the gray subtle print, cut:
- 4 strips, each 1" x 42", for middle borders

From the black subtle print, cut:
- 4 strips, each 3½" x 42", for outer borders

From the yellow-orange mottled print, cut:
- 5 strips, each 2" x 42", for binding

Note: *Refer to "Basic Quiltmaking Techniques" on pages 9–16 for guidance as needed.*

Constructing the Moon

1. With right sides together and long raw edges aligned, sew 42"-long yellow- and orange-print strips of varying widths together in a random, visually pleasing arrangement to make a strip set approximately 16" x 42". (You'll have some strips left over.) Press the seams to one side.

2. Crosscut the newly pieced fabric into strips as follows: 3 strips, each 1" x 16"; 3 strips, each 1½" x 16"; 3 strips, each 2" x 16"; 3 strips, each 2½" x 16"; and 3 strips, each 3" x 16". Set the rest of the strip set aside.

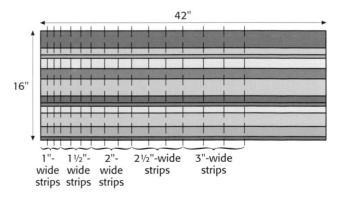

3. Randomly arrange the strips from step 2 beside each other, aligning the long raw edges as shown on page 58. Change the direction of each alternate strip, and occasionally trim and insert a leftover 1" to 3" unpieced strip for variety.

4. With right sides together and long raw edges aligned, begin sewing the strips together. Press the seams to one side. Continue sewing pieced and unpieced strips until the new fabric panel measures approximately 16" x 20".

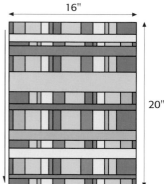

5. Use a yardstick compass to mark an arc of approximately 16" on the fabric panel from step 4. Cut out the arc directly on the marked line.

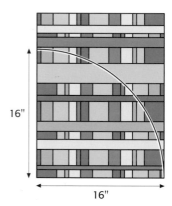

Tip

If you don't have a yardstick compass, make a knot in one end of a piece of household cord. Run a large-headed quilter's pin through the knot. Cut the cord to a length of approximately 16½" and tie the cut end around a pencil or other marking tool.

Spread the newly-pieced fabric on a carpet or other "pinnable" surface. Insert the tip of the pin into the lower-left corner of the fabric. Pull the cord taut, and mark an arc from the top left edge of the fabric to lower-right edge. You'll have the 16" arc you need for the moon.

6. Cut a 3½" x 16" strip from the leftover panel from step 5. Turn this strip lengthwise, and sew it to the straight left edge of the arc from step 5. Trim if necessary; press.

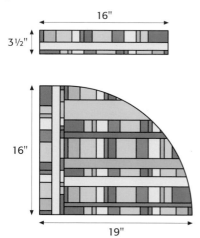

7. To make the craters in the moon, fold each 6" yellow solid square diagonally in both directions to find its center. Unfold, and then place each of the squares randomly on the moon arc as shown, right sides together. Use a compass to draw a circle with a 2" diameter in the center of each yellow square.

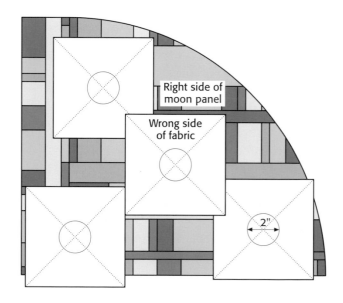

8. Use matching thread to sew each circle directly on the marked line. Cut out each circle through all layers, leaving a ¼"-wide seam allowance. Clip the seam allowance, and turn the yellow square through the hole to the reverse side of the moon arc; press. Pin the outer edges of the square to the arc to secure them before proceeding.

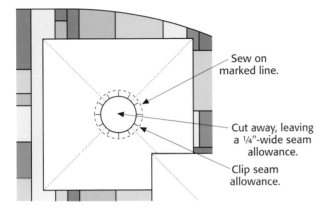

Sew on marked line.

Cut away, leaving a ¼"-wide seam allowance.

Clip seam allowance.

9. Using the moon arc as a template, mark and cut an arc of the same size from the remaining yellow solid fabric. Pin the 2 arcs right sides together, and stitch a ¼"-wide seam along the curved edge only. Turn the unit right side out, and press.

Assembling the Quilt Top

1. Refer to the quilt photo on page 56. Pin the moon unit to lower-left corner of the 37" x 27" piece of black star background print, pieced side up, making sure to align the lower-left corners. Use matching thread to hand appliqué the curved edge of the moon to the background fabric. Do not trim the background fabric from under the appliqué; you'll do that later, after the borders are attached.

2. Transfer the udder (A), cow-body (B), and cow-head (C) appliqué patterns on page 62 to the paper side of a piece of freezer paper. Use a dry iron to press the cow-body and cow-head paper patterns waxy side down to the right side of white fabric scraps and the udder pattern to a pink fabric scrap.

3. Leaving the paper in place, cut out the fabric shapes, adding a ¼"-wide seam allowance. Refer to the photos on page 56 and at upper right and pin the

appliqués in place so the cow appears to be jumping over the moon. Working in alphabetical order (udder, body, head), use matching thread to appliqué the pieces to the background fabric. Use the edges of the paper as a guide for turning the raw edges.

4. Remove the freezer paper and use a fine-point black permanent marker to draw facial features and other details on the cow, or use embroidery stitches if you prefer. Refer to the pattern and the photo below for guidance as needed.

5. Sew the borders to the quilt top, referring to "Adding Borders" on page 11.

Assembly Diagram

6. Carefully trim the black background fabric from behind the moon arc appliqué, leaving a ¼"-wide seam allowance.

Layering, Quilting, and Binding

1. Center and layer the quilt top over the batting and backing; baste.

2. Quilt as desired by hand or machine. The moon craters are quilted through all layers, approximately 1½" from the edge of each hole.

3. Use the 2" x 42" yellow-orange mottled-print strips to make the binding. Sew the binding to the quilt. Trim the batting and backing even with the edges of the quilt top. Blindstitch to secure the binding.

4. Make a label and attach it to your quilt.

Making the Dolls, Animals, and Moveable Toys

1. Using the photo on page 56 for guidance, sew 8 buttons to the quilt for attaching various flat toys. Remember to attach all buttons securely and keep the quilt away from children under age 3.

2. Refer to the instructions and photos indicated by page number, and use the appropriate fabrics, scraps, and notions to make the following dolls and toys:

    *   Button-on sun (page 45), planet Earth (page 45), Uranus (page 45), Saturn (page 46), spaceship (page 46), and UFO (page 47). Attach these items by buttoning them to the quilt as desired.

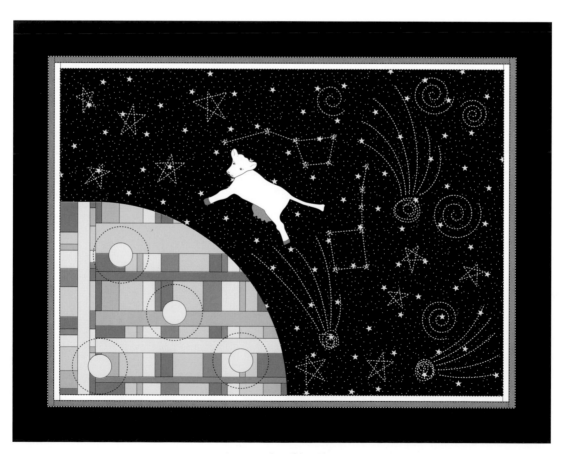

Suggested Quilting Plan

- One each of the girl and boy pilot dolls (page 18) and 2 moon people dolls (page 18). Place the pilot dolls in the windows of the spaceship and the moon people in 2 of the moon craters.

- Two mice (page 34). Place the mice in the remaining 2 moon craters.

Making and Attaching the Moon-and-Half-Sun Trim

YOU'LL NEED 6 moons and 5 half-suns for the dimensional trim on this quilt.

Use leftover strip-pieced fabric from constructing the moon (step 1, page 57) for the front of each shape and leftover yellow solid fabric for the backs. Do not make buttonholes in these finished shapes.

> ## *Tip*
>
> **If you need additional strip-pieced fabric, make it with strips left from piecing the original strip set.**

1. Refer to the instructions for the "Animal Train" moon (page 49). Using the pattern on page 55, make 3 regular and 3 reverse moons. (Make the reverse moons by flipping the template before tracing.)

2. Refer to the instructions for the "Animal Train" sun (page 48). To make the half-suns, trace the border sun pattern (page 50) and the ray pattern (page 55) onto your preferred template material. Cut out the templates.

3. Trace and cut 40 ray pieces from remaining scraps of the yellow-orange mottled binding fabric. Place rays right sides together in pairs, and sew the 2 sides indicated on the pattern. Trim the tip, and turn each ray right side out. (See box top right.)

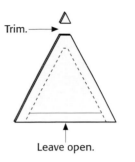

Note: *Instead of pivoting, stitch 1 or 2 stitches across top of ray to get a sharper point when turning.*

Trim.

Leave open.

4. Trace the sun template onto a remaining scrap of strip-pieced fabric and cut, adding a ¼"-wide seam allowance. Repeat to cut a total of 3 suns. Cut each sun in half. Set 1 half aside for another project.

5. Repeat step 4 to trace and cut a total of 3 suns (6 halves) from a remaining scrap of yellow solid fabric. Set 1 half aside.

6. Cut a 4" x 6" piece of batting and place it on your work surface. Center a yellow solid half-sun over it right side up. Space and pin 4 rays around the curved edge of the sun, aligning the raw edges of the rays with the raw edges of the curve. Point the tips inward. Finish the sandwich with a strip-pieced half-sun, right side down.

7. Sew all around the half-sun with a ¼"-wide seam, leaving a small opening along the straight edge for turning. Trim the batting even with the raw edges of the fabric shape.

8. Clip the seam allowance if necessary, and turn the half sun right side out; press. Use matching thread to close the opening with a blind or ladder stitch.

9. Repeat steps 6 through 8 to layer, stitch, turn, and finish the remaining 4 half-sun units.

10. Refer to the photo on page 56. Beginning with back-to-back moons in the upper-right corner, pin alternating moons and half-suns as shown. Use matching thread to hand stitch them to the quilt binding.

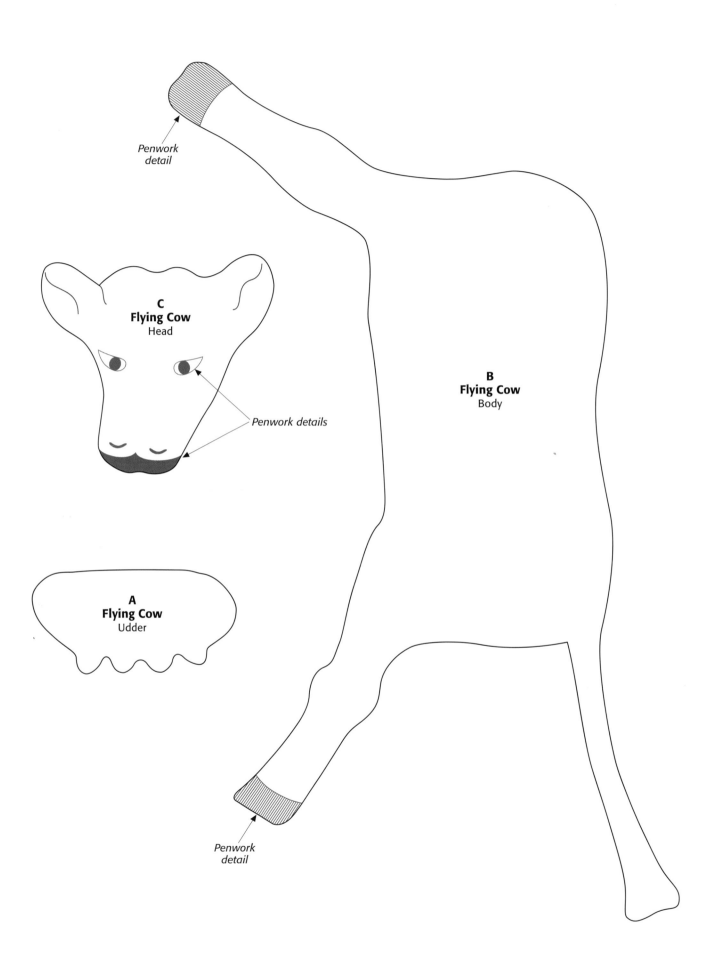

Penwork
detail

C
Flying Cow
Head

Penwork details

B
Flying Cow
Body

A
Flying Cow
Udder

Penwork
detail

Pirate Ship

Pirate Ship by Kristin Kolstad Addison, 1999, Førde, Norway.

Finished quilt size: 53" x 40"
Dolls: pirate, little girl in the red dress, little boy, mermaid
One-Piece Animals: 5 fish, devil ray, 3 seagulls, dolphin, tiger shark, octopus
Moveable Flat Toys: rowboat

Materials

42"-wide fabric

- 1⅜ yd. light blue print for sky
- ¼ yd. *each* of 6 assorted medium to dark blue, green, and turquoise prints for sea
- ⅝ yd. red subtle print for borders
- ½ yd. black solid or subtle print for binding
- 2½ yds. fabric for backing
- Assorted scraps for starfish appliqués, boathouse and wharf, pirate ship, treasure bag, sun, and oyster
- ½ yd. muslin for backings for boathouse, pirate ship, and pirate-ship sails
- Fabric scraps and assorted notions for dolls, animals, and moveable toys*
- 58" x 45" piece of batting
- Small scraps of fusible web
- Batting scraps for fixed items
- 15" length of ½"-wide gold silky ribbon or trim for wharf swing
- Fine-point gold and black permanent markers for details
- 1¼ yds. total of ⅜"-wide satin ribbon in various colors for loops
- Scrap of fine gold ribbon or cord for treasure bag
- Assorted beads for jewels
- 2 gold buttons for attaching sun
- 1 large "pearl" for the oyster
- 15–20 assorted theme-related buttons for hanging flat toys, decoration
- 8" x 15" piece of gold netting for fish net (optional)
- ½ yd. very narrow gold ribbon or cording for fish net (optional)

* See instructions for specific doll, animal, or toy for fabrics and notions required.

Cutting

All measurements include ¼"-wide seam allowances.

From the light blue print, cut:
- 1 piece, 46" x 20", for sky

From *each* of the 6 assorted blue, green, and turquoise prints, cut:
- 2 strips, each 2¼" x 42" (total 12 strips). Subcut each strip into 18 squares, each 2¼" x 2¼" (total 216 squares), for sea.**

From the red subtle print, cut:
- 5 strips, each 4" x 42", for borders

From the black solid or subtle print, cut:
- 5 strips, each 3" x 42", for binding

** You'll have 8 squares left over.

Note: *Refer to "Basic Quiltmaking Techniques" on pages 9–16 for guidance as needed.*

Assembling the Quilt Top

1. Arrange 208 of the 2¼" assorted blue, green, and turquoise squares in 26 vertical rows of 8 squares each, beginning with the lighter squares on the left and moving to the darker on the right, as shown.

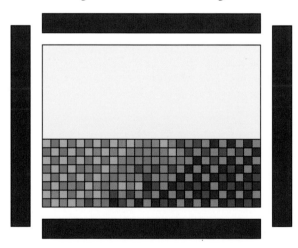

2. Refer to "Quick Chain Piecing" on page 10. Sew the squares into a single unit; press. The pieced unit should measure 46" x 14½".

3. With right sides together and long raw edges aligned, pin and sew the top edge of the pieced sea unit to the bottom edge of the 46" x 20" blue sky piece. Refer to the photo for guidance as needed. Press the seam toward the sky piece.

4. Sew the 4" x 42" red border strips end to end to make a continuous 4"-wide border. Measure the quilt

through its horizontal center and cut 2 borders to that measurement. Sew these borders to the top and bottom of the quilt and press the seam allowance toward the borders.

5. Measure the quilt through its vertical center, including the borders just added. Cut 2 strips to that measurement from the remaining 4"-wide red border strip and sew them to opposite sides of the quilt; press.

6. Refer to "Fusible Appliqué" on page 11, and use the pattern on page 70 to trace and cut 7 starfish from various brightly colored print scraps. Fuse the starfish to the quilt, referring to the photo on page 63 for guidance as needed.

Layering, Quilting, and Binding

1. Divide the backing fabric crosswise into 2 equal panels of approximately 45" each. Remove the selvages and join the pieces to make a single backing panel.

2. Position the backing so that the seam runs vertically. Center and layer the quilt top and the batting over the backing; baste.

3. I quilted my quilt by hand, but you may quilt by hand or machine as desired.

Suggested Quilting Plan

4. Use the 3" x 42" black fabric strips to make the binding. Sew the binding to the quilt. Trim the batting and backing even with the quilt top. Blindstitch to secure the binding.

5. Make a label and attach it to your quilt.

Making the Fixed Items

THE FIXED items on this quilt consist of a boathouse, wharf, pirate ship with sails, treasure bag with jewels, sun, and an oyster with a pearl.

Refer to the photo on page 63 for guidance when sewing the fixed items to the quilt. Use thread in a matching color to blindstitch each piece in place.

Boathouse

The boathouse is constructed of 3 separate pieces: the roof, the house, and the stone wall.

1. To make the roof, cut one 3" x 7" piece from a green-print scrap for the roof and another from muslin for the backing. Cut a slightly larger piece of batting. Follow the instructions for the basic moveable flat toy, steps 1 though 5 (page 45).

2. To make the house, cut one 3" x 5½" piece *each* from a brown-print scrap (house) and muslin (backing), and a slightly larger piece of batting. Follow the instructions for the basic moveable flat toy, steps 1 through 5 (page 45).

3. To make the stone wall, follow the instructions for the basic moveable flat toy, steps 1 through 5 (page 45). Use the stone-wall pattern on page 70, a gray "stone"-print scrap for the wall, and muslin for the backing.

4. Place the house unit and the stone-wall unit right sides together, aligning the bottom edge of the house with the top edge of the wall. Also align the left edges. Use matching-colored thread to whipstitch the units together.

5. Lay the roof face down on your work surface. Center the unit from step 4 face down over the roof, overlapping the bottom edge by approximately 1". Use matching thread to whipstitch the unit from step 4 to the roof.

6. Refer to the photo on page 63. Turn the completed boathouse unit face up and hand sew it to the quilt, overlapping the border as shown. Leave the right edge of the roof and house unattached to form a pocket.

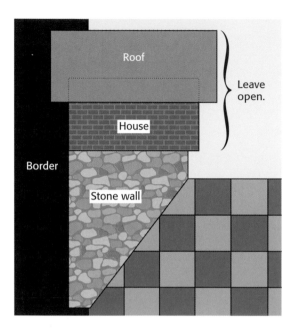

Wharf

The wharf consists of 2 separate pieces: the dock and the piling.

1. For the dock, cut a 1½" x 20" strip from a brown "woody"-print scrap. Fold the fabric in half length-wise, right sides together, matching the long raw edges.

2. Stitch approximately ½" from the long folded edge, all along the length of the strip. Leave the short ends open.

3. Use a safety pin to turn the strip right side out. Press flat with seam on one edge.

4. Close the short ends with matching thread and a blind or ladder stitch.

5. For the piling, cut one 2½" x 10" strip from a complementary brown "woody"-print scrap and another from lightweight batting. Fold the fabric in half lengthwise, right sides together, matching the long raw edges.

6. Stitch all along the length of the strip with a ¼"-wide seam allowance. Leave the short ends open.

7. Use a safety pin to turn the piling strip right side out. Center the seam on the underside and press. Roll the batting strip lengthwise, and use the safety pin to coax the rolled batting into the piling to stuff it.

8. Close the short ends with matching thread and a blind or ladder stitch.

9. To attach the wharf to the quilt, fold the dock strip in half and crease to mark its center point. Place one end of the dock, seam side facing the bottom edge of the quilt, just inside the boathouse "pocket." Tuck the 2 ends of a 15" piece of ½"-wide gold ribbon or trim about ¾" apart under the dock between the boathouse and the crease as shown. Pin the dock and the ribbon to secure, and use matching thread and a blind stitch to sew the dock to the quilt along its top and bottom edges. Be sure to catch the ends of the ribbon in your stitches. Stop sewing when you reach the crease, and remove the pins.

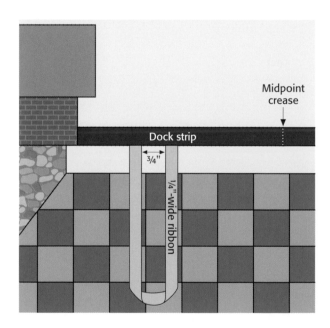

10. Fold the remaining dock strip back over itself and tack at 3" intervals, leaving pockets for toys.

11. Refer to the photo on page 63. Place the piling, seam side down, approximately 1" from the far end of the dock and extending a little bit above the dock, as shown. Use matching thread and a blind stitch to hand sew it in place.

Pirate Ship

The pirate ship consists of 11 separate pieces: a hull, 6 sails (A–F), a flag, and 3 mast segments.

1. To make the hull, follow the instructions for the basic moveable flat toy, steps 1 through 5 (page 45). Use the hull patterns on pages 72–73 (joining the halves as indicated), a brown "woody"-print scrap for the hull, and muslin for the backing. Quilt a few "board" lines on the hull, as indicated on the pattern.

2. Use a scrap of the same brown "woody" print to make the mast. Follow the instructions for the wharf piling, steps 5 through 7 (page 66), using one 1½" x 25" strip each of the brown fabric and batting. Cut the completed mast into 3 lengths, 5", 7", and 11", and close the short ends of each segment with a blind or ladder stitch in matching thread.

3. Follow the instructions for the basic moveable flat toy, steps 1 through 5 (page 45), to make 1 each of sail A through sail F. Use the sail patterns on pages 70–73 and muslin for both the sail fronts and backings. I use a very soft batting in the sails to make them pillowy.

4. Use black scraps to make both the front and back sides of the pirate flag. Follow the instructions for the basic moveable flat toy, steps 1 through 5 (page 45), and use the flag pattern on page 70. Finish by drawing a "Jolly Roger" (skull and crossbones) on the front side of the flag with a fine-point permanent marker. I prefer to make the flag without batting.

5. Refer to the diagram above right and the photo on page 63. Use matching thread and a blind stitch to sew the 3 masts and the pirate-ship hull to the quilt. Sew the masts along the long edges and the hull on the sides and bottom only. Sew together the masts and hull where they meet.

6. Attach the 6 sails by tacking them at the corners and add the flag by stitching along the edge closest to the mast.

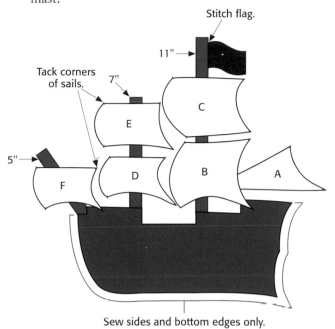

Stitch flag.

Tack corners of sails.

11"

7"

5"

Sew sides and bottom edges only.

Treasure Bag and Jewels

1. Cut a 3" x 7" scrap of black fabric. Sew a ¼"-wide double-fold hem along one long side. Fold the fabric in half, right sides together, matching the 2 short raw edges.

2. Leaving the hemmed side open, sew the 2 remaining unsewn sides (1 short, 1 long) with a ¼"-wide seam. Clip the corners, turn the bag right side out, and press.

3. Tack a length of gold ribbon or cord around the outside edge of the bag, 1" below the hemmed opening. Knot the ends.

4. Fill the bag with pre-strung beads and other "jewels." If you prefer, string your own on strong quilting or beading thread.

5. Refer to the photo on page 63 and use matching thread to tack the treasure bag to the ocean floor.

Refer to the photo on page 63

Sun

1. Trace the sun and ray patterns (pages 72) onto your preferred template material. Cut out the templates.

2. Trace and cut 10 ray pieces *each* from scraps of yellow-checked fabric and scraps of yellow subtle-print fabric, adding a ¼"-wide seam allowance to each piece. Place matching rays right sides together

in pairs and sew the 2 sides indicated on the pattern, stitching on the drawn lines. Trim the tip and turn each ray right side out.

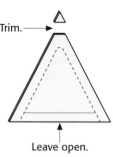
3. Trace the sun template twice onto a scrap of yellow-checked fabric. Cut out each piece, adding a ¼"-wide seam allowance.

4. Cut a 4" square of batting and place it on your work surface. Center 1 yellow-checked sun over it right side up. Space and pin the rays around the perimeter of the sun, alternating the checked and subtle-print triangles. Align the raw edges of the rays with the raw edges of the circle and point the tips inward. Finish the sandwich with the remaining yellow-checked sun, right side down.

5. Sew around the perimeter of the circle on the drawn line, leaving a small opening for turning as indicated on the pattern. Trim the batting even with the raw edges of the fabric circle, and clip or notch the curves as needed.

6. Turn the sun right side out and press carefully. Hand stitch the opening closed.

7. Refer to the photo on page 63 and stitch the sun to the quilt with 2 gold button "eyes."

Refer to the photo on page 63

Oyster with Pearl

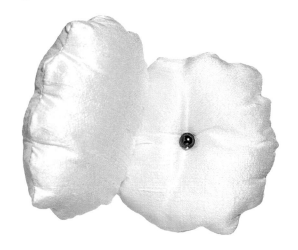

Note: *Although this toy is technically constructed in 2 pieces, you will make it using the instructions for the basic one-piece animal.*

1. Follow steps 1 through 4 in the instructions for the basic one-piece animal (pages 33–34). Use the pattern on page 71 and white or gray-solid or subtle-print scraps for both the front and back of the shell. Stuff with a little less batting than usual. Repeat to make a second shell.

2. Turn in the opening on both shells and use matching thread and a single seam to close the openings and stitch the 2 shells together along the short, turned edge.

3. Quilt a few scallop lines on each shell and stitch a large "pearl" to one of the halves.

4. Refer to the photo on page 63 and use matching thread to tack the oyster to the ocean floor.

Making the Dolls, Animals, and Moveable Toys

1. Using the photo on page 63 for guidance, sew 15–20 theme-related buttons (e.g., fish, stars, anchors, parrots) to the quilt for decoration and for attaching the various animals and moveable flat toys. Remember to attach all buttons securely: this quilt is made for children (ages 3 and older) to play with!

2. Refer to the instructions and photos indicated by page number and use the appropriate fabrics, scraps, and notions to make the following dolls, toys, and animals:

   - One each of the pirate (page 19), little girl in the red dress (page 20), little boy (page 21), and mermaid (page 21). Place the pirate in a sail or pocket in the hull of the pirate ship and the mermaid in the gold-ribbon swing dangling from the wharf. The little girl and boy can be slipped into pockets to stand on the dock.

   - Five fish (page 34), 1 devil ray (page 34), 3 seagulls (page 35), and 1 each of the dolphin (page 35), tiger shark (page 35), and octopus (page 35). Attach these items by buttoning them to the quilt as desired.

   - One sunken rowboat (page 47). Attach the boat by buttoning it to the quilt.

Tip

Make a fishnet to hold a fish or two—or all of the toys, if you wish. Follow the instructions for making the treasure bag on page 67. Substitute an 8" x 15" piece of gold netting for the bag and a ½ yard of narrow gold cording for the tie. Leave a small opening in the hem and run the cord through to make a drawstring. Sew a large, gold, nautical-style button to the stern (rear!) of the pirate ship, and loop the knotted cording over it to hold the net in place.

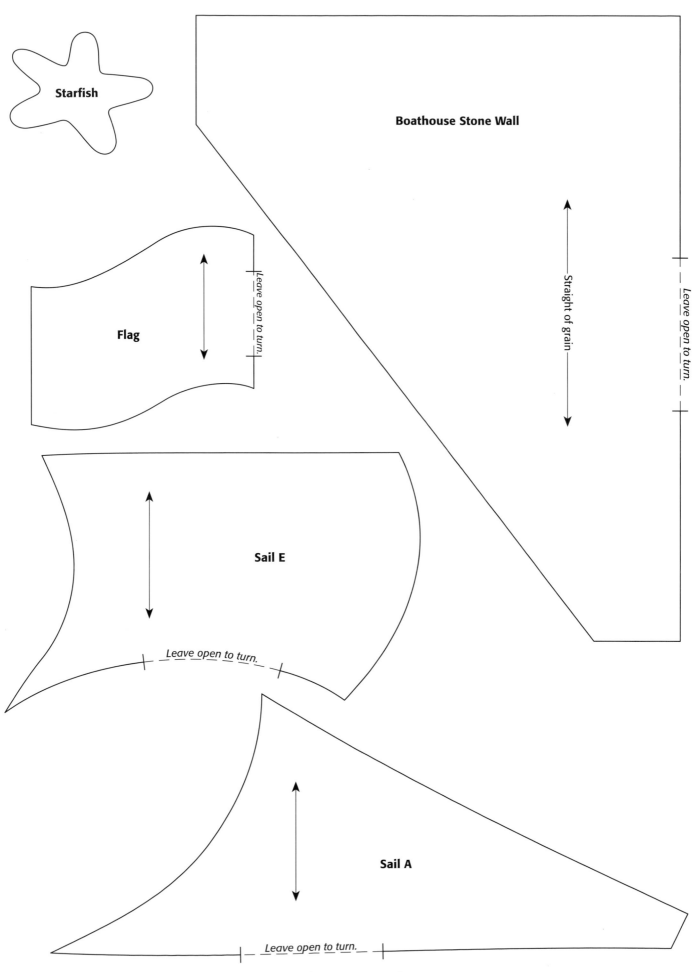

Starfish

Boathouse Stone Wall

Straight of grain

Leave open to turn.

Flag

Leave open to turn.

Sail E

Leave open to turn.

Sail A

Leave open to turn.

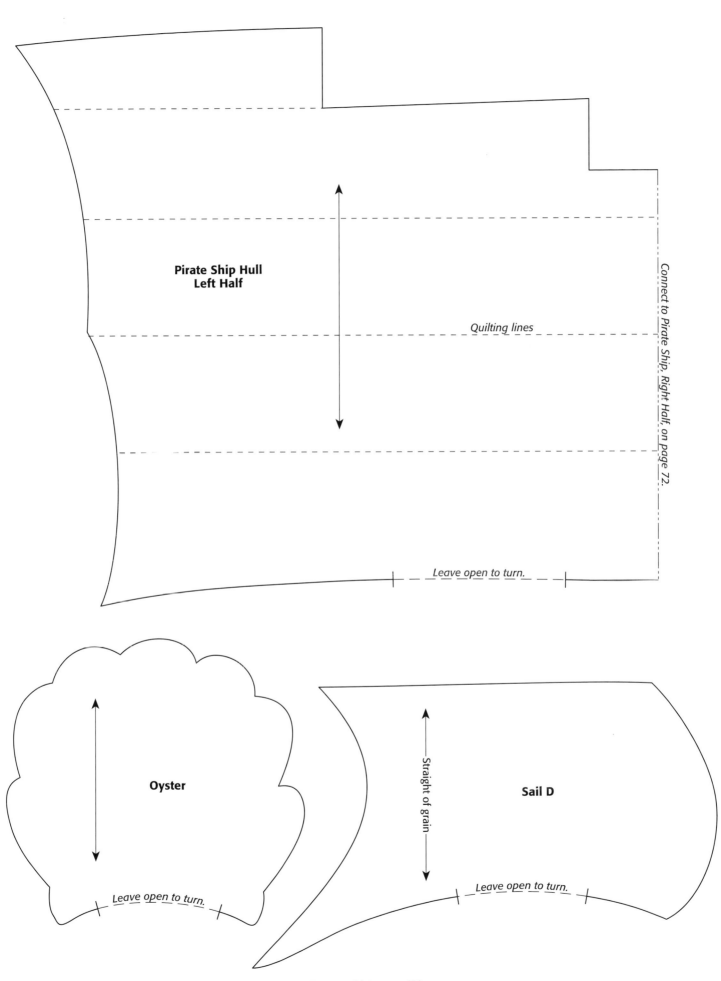

**Pirate Ship Hull
Left Half**

Quilting lines

Connect to Pirate Ship, Right Half, on page 72.

Leave open to turn.

Oyster

Leave open to turn.

Straight of grain

Sail D

Leave open to turn.

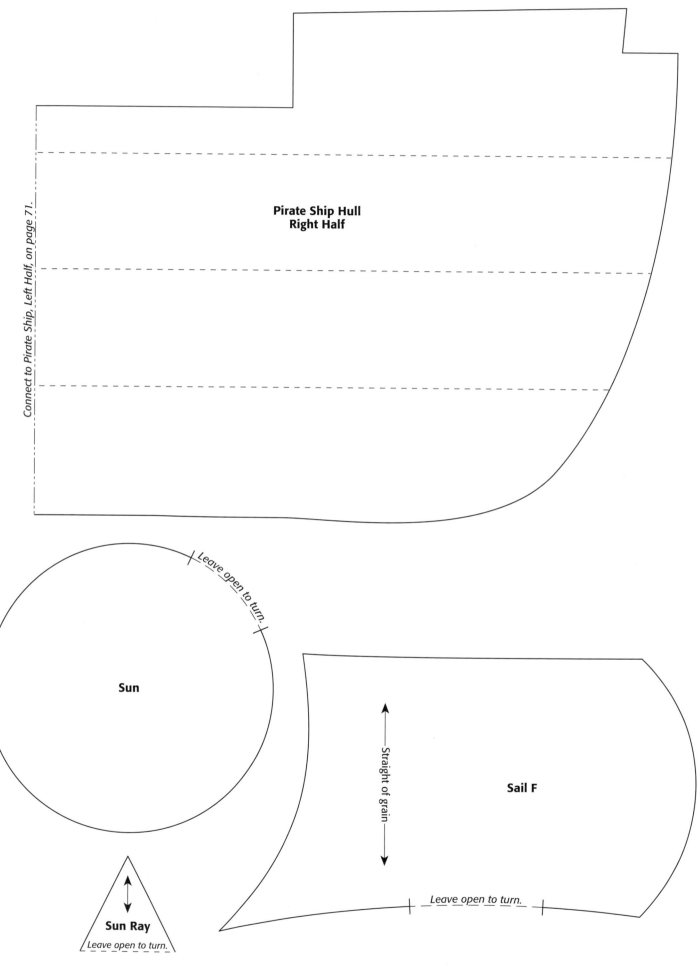

**Pirate Ship Hull
Right Half**

Connect to Pirate Ship, Left Half, on page 71.

Leave open to turn.

Sun

Straight of grain

Sail F

Leave open to turn.

Sun Ray

Leave open to turn.

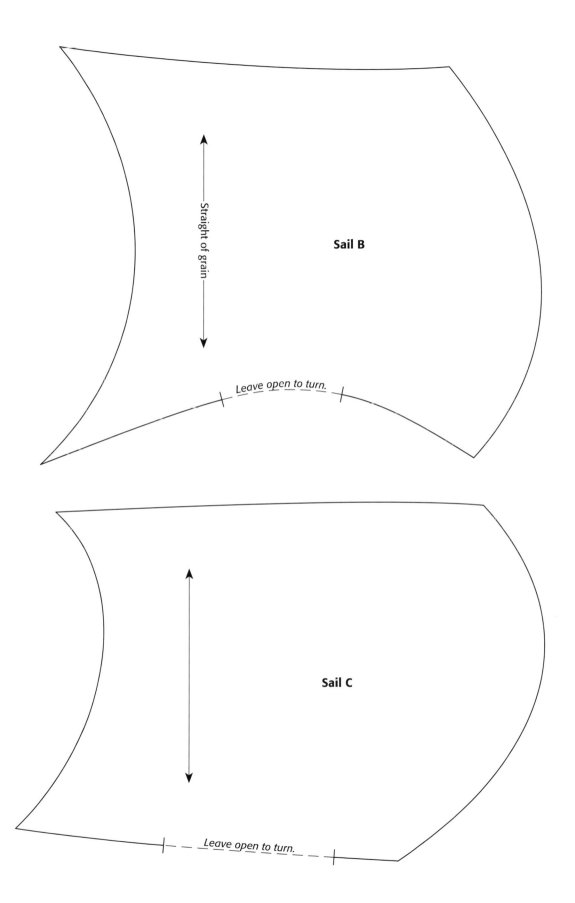

Sail B

Straight of grain

Leave open to turn.

Sail C

Leave open to turn.

On the Farm (E-I-E-I-O!)

On the Farm (E-I-E-I-O!) by Kristin Kolstad Addison, 2000, Førde, Norway.

Finished quilt size: 57" x 51½" (approximate)
Dolls: farm girl and farm boy
One-Piece Animals: cow, calf, pig #1, pig #2, 2 piglets, horse, cat, 3 hens
Moveable Flat Toys: scarecrow

Materials

42"-wide fabric

- Fat quarter brown #1 for barn bridge
- ⅜ yd. red print for barn
- ⅝ yd. light blue print for sky
- Fat quarter black print for barn roof*
- ⅜ yd. muslin for barn side wall lining, inner roof, and hayloft doors
- Fat quarter brown print #2 for inner barn wall*
- Fat quarter brown print #3 for barn floor and hayloft*
- Scrap of brown print #4 for barn floor braces
- ⅝ yd. green print for grass
- Fat quarter each of 3 different green prints for field*
- Fat quarter each of 2 different brown prints for field*
- ½ yd. red plaid for inner border
- 1 yd. farmyard print for outer border
- 3½ yds. fabric for backing
- Assorted fabric scraps for barn bridge, tree, leaves, well, hammock, field, tractor, beehive, sun, and clouds
- Fabric scraps and assorted notions for dolls, animals, and moveable toys**
- 61" x 55" piece of batting
- Batting scraps for fixed items
- 3 large black buttons for tractor
- 20" length of ⅛"–wide black satin ribbon for hammock
- 8" length of ⅛"–wide red satin ribbon for hayloft
- Assorted blue seed and bugle beads for rain-drops
- Beading needle and thread
- 20–25 assorted utility and theme-related buttons for hanging animals and flat toys and for decoration
- 2½ yds. of ⅜"-wide silk ribbon in different colors for hanging loops
- 2 ready-made goose appliqués (optional)

* *Leftover scraps can be used for animals, fixed items, etc.*

** *See instructions for specific doll, animal, or toy for fabrics and notions required.*

Cutting

All cutting measurements include ¼"-wide seam allowances.

From brown print #1, cut:
- 2 strips, each 4½" x 12", for barn bridge

From the red print, cut:
- 1 piece, 10½" x 9⅛" for barn (A)
- 1 strip, 10½" x 4½", for front barn wall
- 1 strip, 14" x 7", for side barn wall (flap)

From the light blue print, cut:
- 1 square, 5⅞" x 5⅞". Cut square once diagonally to make 2 triangles (B) for sky
- 2 pieces, each 9" x 8½" (C), for sky
- 1 strip, 41" x 8½" (E), for sky

From the black print, cut:
- 1 strip, 8½" x 1½", for barn roof
- 2 strips, each 19" x 5½", for barn roof and lining

From the muslin, cut:
- 1 strip, 14" x 7", for barn side wall (flap) lining
- 1 strip, 19" x 5½", for inner barn roof
- 1 strip, 14 x 4½", for barn floor

From brown print #2, cut:
- 1 strip, 14" x 7", for inner side barn wall

From brown print #3, cut:
- 1 strip, 14" x 4½", for barn floor

From brown print #4, cut:
- 2 squares, each 4⅜" x 4⅜", for barn floor braces. Cut each square once diagonally to make a total of 4 triangles.

From the green print, cut:
- 2 strips, each 9" x 4" (D), for grass
- 1 strip, 17" x 7" (F), for grass
- 1 strip, 17" x 2" (G), for grass
- 1 piece, 14" x 16" (H), for grass
- 1 piece, 11" x 16"(I), for grass

From the 3 different green prints, cut a *total* of:
- 1 strip, 4" x 17", for field
- 1 strip, 4⅞" x 17", for field
- 1 strip, 2⅞" x 17", for field

From the 2 different brown prints, cut a *total* of:
- 1 strip, 4½" x 17", for field
- 1 strip, 3⅞" x 17", for field

From the red plaid, cut:
- 4 strips, each 3" x 42", for inner border

From the farmyard print, cut:
- 5 strips, each 6" x 42", for outer border

Note: *Refer to "Basic Quiltmaking Techniques" on pages 9–16 for guidance as needed.*

Raising the Barn

1. Use a rotary cutter and ruler to trim opposite corners of each 4½" x 12" brown-print-#1 strip along the bias at a 45° angle as shown. Refer to "Cutting Accurate Strips," step 7 (page 10) for guidance as needed.

Cut 1 of each.

2. Place the trimmed brown strips right sides together and sew the 2 long sides and 1 short side with a ¼"-wide seam. Clip the corners, turn the unit right side out, and press to make the bridge.

3. Measure across the top (10½") edge of the 10½" x 9⅛" red print A piece to find and mark its midpoint. Measure and mark 3⅞" from both the lower-left and lower-right corners as well. Use your rotary cutter and ruler to connect the markings on the sides and top of the piece. Cut off the upper corner triangles as shown.

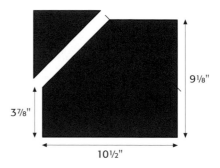

Lay the trimmed A piece right side up on your work surface. Place the bridge unit from step 2 right sides together with A, matching the center point of piece A with the center point of the raw edge of the bridge as shown.

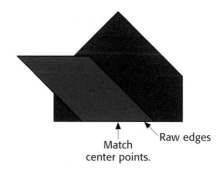

Match center points.

Raw edges

4. Place the 10½" x 4½" red-print strip right sides together with the unit from step 3, aligning the long raw edges. Sew the long raw edge with a ¼"-wide seam. Open the unit as shown, and press as desired.

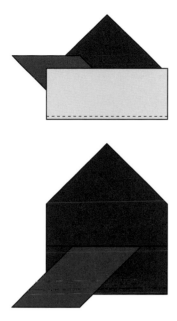

5. Fold the 8½" x 1½" black print strip in half, wrong sides together, aligning the long raw edges, and press. Refer to the photo on page 76 and the diagram below. With right sides together, sew a blue-print triangle (B) to the unit from step 4, inserting the raw edge of the folded black strip in the seam as shown. Press the seams away from the triangle. Set this unit aside.

6. To make the side wall, layer a 15" x 8" piece of batting, the 14" x 7" red-print strip (right side up), and the 14" x 7" muslin strip. Sew the 2 short sides and 1 long side with a ¼"-wide seam. Trim the excess batting, clip the corners, turn the unit right side out, and press.

7. Starting from the long, finished edge, hand or machine quilt parallel lines (1" apart) on the unit from step 6. Stop quilting approximately 1½" inches from the long raw edge.

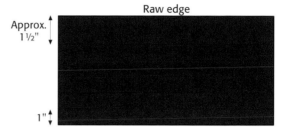

8. To make the roof, refer to step 1 and trim the corners from the 19" x 5½" muslin inner roof strip and the two 19" x 5½" black-print roof strips at a 45° angle as shown. Set the black pieces aside for now.

Cut 1 black.

Cut 1 black and 1 muslin.

9. To make the hay loft, refer to step 5 and sew the remaining blue-print triangle (B) to the right diagonal edge of the trimmed muslin roof strip from step 8. Press the seam allowance toward the triangle, and set the unit aside for now.

10. Layer the 14" x 7" brown-print-#2 strip (right-side up), the wall unit from step 7 (red print side up), and the unit from step 9 (wrong side up) as shown, aligning the long raw edges. Sew through all 5 layers, open the unit, and press.

11. Layer a 5" square of batting and 2 brown-print-#4 triangles (right sides together). Sew the diagonal and 1 short straight side of the triangles with a ¼" seam allowance as shown to make a barn floor brace. Trim the excess batting even with the raw edges of the fabric, clip the corners, turn the piece right side out, and press. Repeat for the second floor brace unit.

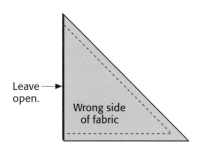

Leave open.

Wrong side of fabric

12. Lay the unit from step 10 right side up on your work surface. Align the raw edge of 1 floor brace unit from step 11 with the lower-left corner of the larger unit as shown. (Pin the red-and-muslin flap out of the way so you do not catch it in the seam.) Aligning the bottom edges, add the unit from step 5, wrong side up. Sew the layers together with a ¼"-wide seam, stopping and pivoting at the roofline as shown. Open the unit and press as desired.

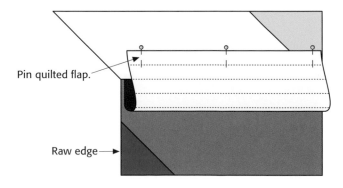

Pin quilted flap.

Raw edge

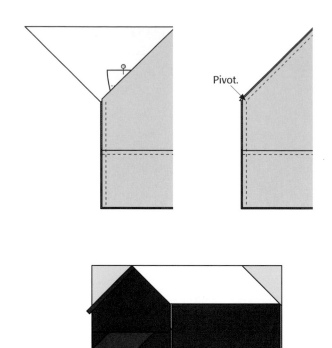

Pivot.

13. To make the floor unit, layer a 15" x 6" piece of batting, the 14" x 4½" brown-print-#3 strip (right side up), and the 14" x 4½" muslin strip. Sew the 2 short sides and 1 long side with a ¼"-wide seam. Trim the excess batting, clip the corners, turn the unit right side out, and press.

14. With right sides together, and aligning the raw edges in the lower right corner, sew the floor unit from step 13 to the bottom edge of the unit from step 12. (Pin the red-and-muslin flap and the floor-brace out of the way so you do not catch them in the seam.) Open the unit; press.

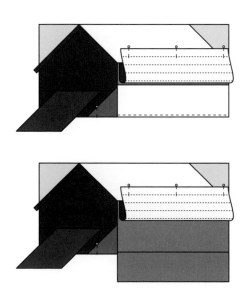

15. Sew a 9" x 8½" blue-print piece C to a 9" x 4" green-print piece D as shown. Press the seams toward D. Make 2.

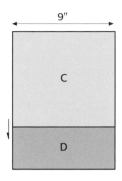

Make 2.

16. Refer to the assembly diagram lower right. Sew 1 unit from step 15 to the left edge of the unit from step 14. Press the seam toward the unit from step 15. Sew the remaining unit from step 15 to the right edge of the unit, inserting the remaining floor brace unit in the seam as you did in step 12. (Pin the red-and-muslin flap, the bridge, and the floor unit out of the way so you do not catch them in the seam.)

17. To make the roof unit, layer a 20" x 7" piece of batting, a black strip reserved from step 8 (right side up), and the remaining black strip (wrong side up). Sew the 2 short sides and 1 long side with a ¼"-wide seam as shown. Trim the excess batting, clip the corners, turn the unit right side out, and press. Quilt with diagonal lines.

18. Lay the unit from step 16 right side up on your work surface. Align the roof unit from step 17 with the inner muslin roof piece in the larger unit, matching raw edges.

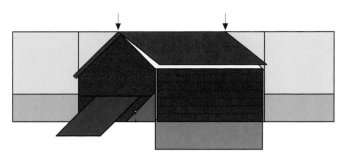

Place the 41" x 8½" blue-print E strip on top of the roof unit, face down, aligning the long raw edges. Sew all layers with a ¼"-wide seam. Open, referring to the assembly diagram as needed, and press as desired.

19. Use matching thread to whipstitch the base of the floor brace triangles to the floor unit. Fold under the front edge of the floor unit.

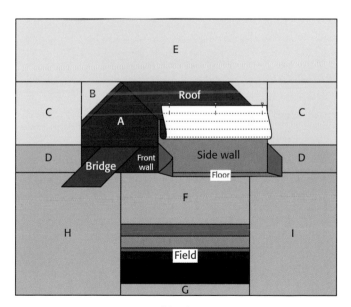

Assembly Diagram

Making the Field

1. Arrange the 17"-long green and brown strips in the following order: 4"-wide green, 4⅞"-wide green, 2⅞"-wide green, 4½"-wide brown, and 3⅞"-wide brown. With right sides together and long raw edges aligned, sew the strips together to make a strip set. Press the seams to one side.

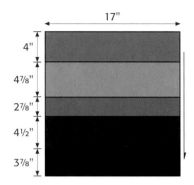

2. Fold the unit from step 1 lengthwise between the seams to make 4 or 5 random-width accordion pleats. Adjust the folds as necessary so that the unit measures 8"; press.

3. Refer to the assembly diagram on page 79 and the photo on page 74. Sew the pleated "field" from step 2 between the 17" x 7" (F) and 17" x 2" (G) green-print strips as shown. (Be sure the brown strip is at the bottom of the field unit!) Press the seams toward the green strips.

4. Sew the unit from step 3 between the 14" x 16" (H) and 11" x 16" (I) green-print strips as shown in the assembly diagram; press.

Assembling the Quilt Top

1. Sew the completed barn unit to the completed field unit as shown in the assembly diagram on page 79. Press the seams toward the bottom unit.

2. Measure the quilt through its horizontal center. Trim two 3" x 42" red plaid inner border strips to that measurement; sew them to the top and bottom of the quilt. Press the seams toward the borders.

3. Measure the quilt through its vertical center, including the borders just added. Trim the remaining 3" x 42" inner border strips to that measurement and sew them to opposite sides of the quilt; press.

4. Sew the 6" x 42" farmyard-print outer border strips end to end to make a continuous 6"-wide border. Measure the quilt through its horizontal center and cut 2 borders to that measurement from the 6"-wide pieced border strip. Sew the borders to the top and bottom of the quilt and press the seams toward the outer borders.

5. Measure the quilt through its vertical center, including the borders just added. Cut 2 borders to that measurement from the remaining 6"-wide pieced farmyard-print border strip and sew them to opposite sides of the quilt; press.

Layering, Quilting, and Finishing the Edges

THIS QUILT does not have ordinary binding. Instead it is layered and finished "pillow-slip" fashion.

1. Divide the backing fabric crosswise into 2 equal panels of approximately 63" each. Remove the selvages and join the pieces to make a single backing panel.

2. Layer the batting and the backing (right side up) and finish the sandwich by centering the quilt top (wrong side up) over both. Pin the layers to secure them.

3. Refer to the photo on page 74 and use a pencil or other fabric marker to draw freehand bows and

curves along the outer edges of the back side of the quilt top. Don't worry if the curves are not perfect; that's part of the fun!

4. Sew directly on the drawn line, all around the perimeter of the quilt top. Trim the backing and batting even with the quilt top. Clip or notch the curves and remove the pins.

5. Use a seam ripper to open approximately 10" of the seam joining the inner and outer borders. Turn the quilt right side out; press.

6. Use matching thread and hand sew the opening closed with a blind or ladder stitch.

7. Pin- or thread-baste the quilt, and then quilt as desired by hand or machine. (I quilted by machine because it was so much fun!)

8. Make a label and attach it to your quilt.

Suggested Quilting Plan

Making the Fixed Items

THE FIXED items on this quilt are a tractor, beehive, well, tree with hammock, hayloft, sun, and clouds.

Refer to the photo on page 74 for guidance in sewing the fixed items to the quilt. Use a blind stitch and thread that matches the pieces.

Tractor

1. Follow the instructions for the basic moveable flat toy, steps 1 through 5 (page 45), using the tractor and wheel patterns on page 85. I used dark blue subtle-print scraps for the front and back of the tractor and black solid scraps for the wheels. Use matching thread to stitch the wheels in place as indicated on the pattern.

2. Refer to the photo above. Fasten the tractor to the quilt by sewing a large black button in the center of each wheel, making sure to catch all layers. Add a button "steering wheel" as indicated on the pattern.

Beehive

1. Follow the instructions for the basic moveable flat toy, steps 1 through 5 (page 45), using the beehive pattern on page 85 and a yellow solid or subtle-print scrap for the front and back of the beehive.

2. Add a few lines of quilting as indicated on the pattern to suggest the rings on the beehive. Attach the hive to the quilt with matching thread and invisible hand stitching.

Well

The well is constructed of 4 separate pieces: the stone base, the roof, and 2 "wooden" support beams.

1. To make the base, cut two 3" x 4" pieces from gray "stone"-print scraps for the front and backing. Cut a slightly larger piece of batting. Layer the batting, one 3" x 4" piece of gray fabric (right side up), and the remaining piece of gray fabric (wrong side up). Machine stitch inside the perimeter of the shape, taking a ¼"-wide seam and leaving a small opening for turning.

2. Trim the excess batting and clip the corners as necessary. Turn the figure right side out; press. Close the opening with a blind or ladder stitch, turning the seam allowance to the inside as you sew.

3. To make the roof, follow the instructions for the basic moveable flat toy, steps 1 through 5 (page 45). Use the well-roof pattern on page 86 and "woody"-print scraps for the front and backing of the roof.

4. To make the support beams, cut one 2" x 6" strip from a brown "woody"-print scrap and another from lightweight batting. Fold the fabric in half with right sides together, lengthwise, matching the long raw edges. Sew along the long raw edge with a ¼"-wide seam. Leave both short ends open.

5. Use a safety pin to turn the strip right side out. Center the seam on the underside and press. (A ¾"-wide bias press bar and a touch of spray starch will help with this step.) Roll the batting strip lengthwise, and use the safety pin to coax the rolled batting into the support beam to stuff it.

6. Cut the completed strip into two 3"-long segments. Referring to the photo at left, use matching thread and invisible stitching to hand sew the beams, roof, and base to the quilt. Sew the base on the sides and bottom only and the roof on the sides and top only.

Tree with Hammock

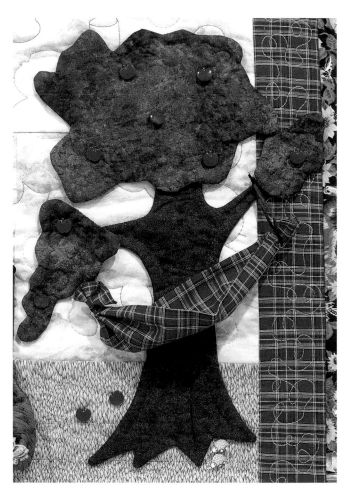

1. To make the tree trunk, follow the instructions for the basic moveable flat toy, steps 1 through 4 (page 45). Use the tree-trunk pattern on page 85 and

brown "woody"-print scraps for the front and backing of the tree. Leave the ends of each limb unsewn.

2. Refer to the photo on page 74. Pin the tree trunk in place and quilt wood-grain lines on the trunk as indicated on the pattern, catching all the layers. Leave the last 2" of the left and right branches free from quilting.

3. To make the leafy tree tops, follow the instructions for the basic moveable flat toy, steps 1 through 5 (page 45). Use the tree-leaf patterns #1, #2, and #3 (pages 86–87) and green-print scraps for the front and backing of each leaf section.

4. To make the hammock, cut an 11" x 10" piece of red-plaid fabric. Fold the fabric in half lengthwise, right sides together, aligning the long edges; press. Sew the raw edges with a ¼"-wide seam, leaving a 3" opening for turning.

5. Clip the corners, turn the hammock right side out, and press. Use matching thread to close the opening with a blind or ladder stitch, turning the seam allowance in as you sew; press again.

6. Cut two 10" lengths of ⅛"-wide black satin ribbon. Gather each short end of the hammock and tie it with a piece of ribbon so it looks like a piece of candy. Wrap the ribbon tails around the left and right tree branches and knot, suspending the hammock in place. Refer to the photo on page 82 for guidance as needed.

7. Pin the 3 leafy tree tops in place. Quilt a few apples or similar motifs on each leafy section. The quilting secures the leafy sections to the tree.

Hayloft

The barn bridge is topped with a double-doored hayloft where the hens like to roost!

1. For each door, cut 2 pieces of muslin, each 3" x 4", and a slightly larger piece of batting. Follow the instructions for the well base (steps 1 and 2, page 82) to construct each door, leaving one 4" side of each door unsewn. Make 2.

2. Use matching thread to hand or machine stitch ⅛"-wide red satin ribbon to each door as shown above.

3. Cut a 5½" x 4" piece from a brown "woody"-print scrap. Turn under a ¼"-wide hem on both 5½" edges and stitch by hand or machine with matching thread.

4. With right sides together and 4" raw edges aligned, sew a door to each short side of the woody brown "wall." Press the seam allowances toward the wall, close the doors, and topstitch close to the edges with thread that matches the door.

5. Pin the hayloft unit to the quilt, just above the barn bridge. Use matching thread and invisible stitches to appliqué the unit to the quilt. Make and sew a silk-ribbon loop on 1 door and add a button to the other for a perfect "latch."

Sun and Clouds

1. To make the sun, follow the instructions for "Pirate Ship" sun (page 68). Use the sun and ray patterns on page 88 and yellow subtle-print scraps for the front and backing of the sun and 5 rays.

2. To make the clouds, follow the instructions for the basic moveable flat toy, steps 1 through 5 (page 45). Use the cloud patterns on page 88 and light blue subtle-print scraps for the front and backing of each cloud.

3. Use matching thread and an invisible stitch to tack the clouds to the sun as shown above.

4. If you wish, string blue seed and bugle beads and stitch the strands to one of the clouds for raindrops.

5. Use matching thread and an invisible stitch to sew the sun-and-cloud unit to the quilt, or if you want the sun and clouds to be moveable, make buttonholes in the sun and clouds and sew corresponding buttons to the quilt.

Making the Dolls, Animals, and Moveable Toys

1. Using the photo on page 74 for guidance, sew 20–25 assorted theme-related buttons (e.g., sunflowers, bees, etc.) to the quilt for decoration and for attaching the various flat toys. Add some apples in the trees and corn and other vegetables in the fields (to help secure the "furrows" in place). Don't forget 3 buttons in the hayloft for the roosting hens! Just remember to attach all buttons securely; this quilt is made for children (ages 3 and older) to play with.

2. Refer to the instructions and photos indicated by page number and use the appropriate fabrics, scraps, and notions to make the following dolls and toys:

   • Three hens (page 37) and scarecrow (page 47). Attach them to the quilt by buttoning them in place.

   • One each of the cow (page 36), calf (page 36), pig #1 (page 36), pig #2 (page 36), 2 piglets (page 36), horse (page 37), and cat (page 37). Place them in the barn, in the furrows in the field, or as desired.

   • One each of the farm girl and farm boy dolls (pages 22–23). Place the little boy in the hammock and the little girl behind the wheel of the tractor.

Finishing Touches

1. Use matching thread and an invisible stitch to secure the short loose end of the barn bridge to the quilt.

2. Make a pair of matching loops from 8" lengths of ⅜"-wide satin ribbon and tack 1 at each end of the side wall lining, just under the side wall flap. Place a button in a corresponding spot just above the side wall flap. Now you can roll up the flap if you wish, and secure it by buttoning the loop. Repeat, if desired, for the roof flap.

3. Refer to the photo on page 74 and add a pair of ready-made, stitch-on goose appliqués, if desired.

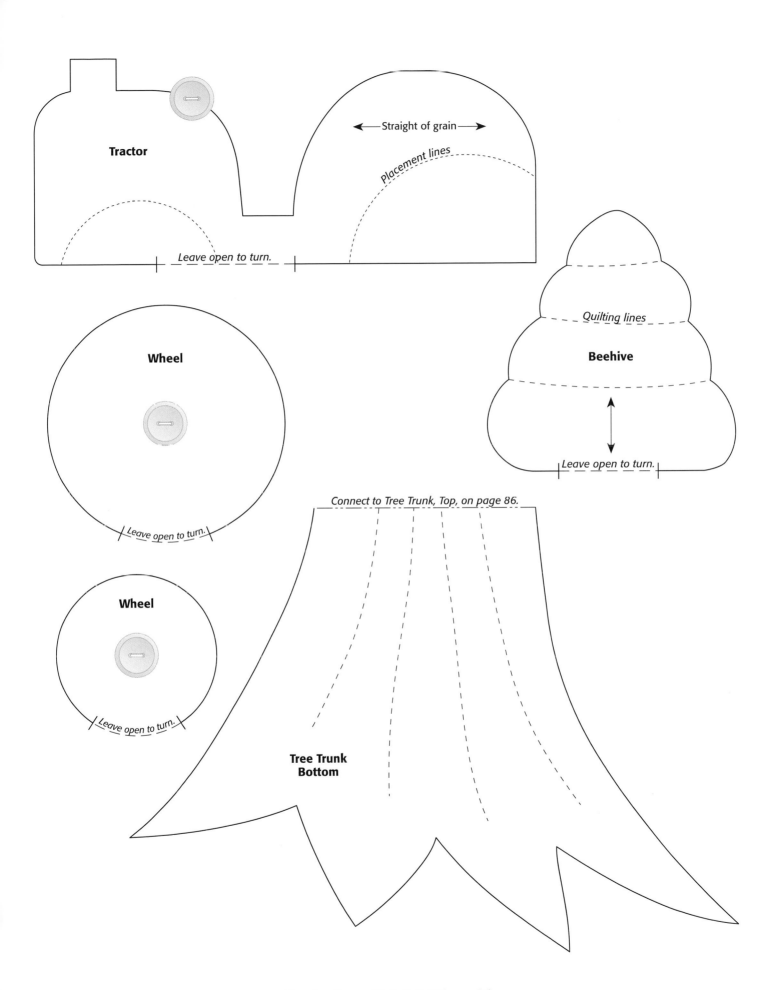

Tractor

Straight of grain

Placement lines

Leave open to turn.

Wheel

Leave open to turn.

Wheel

Leave open to turn.

Quilting lines

Beehive

Leave open to turn.

Connect to Tree Trunk, Top, on page 86.

Tree Trunk Bottom

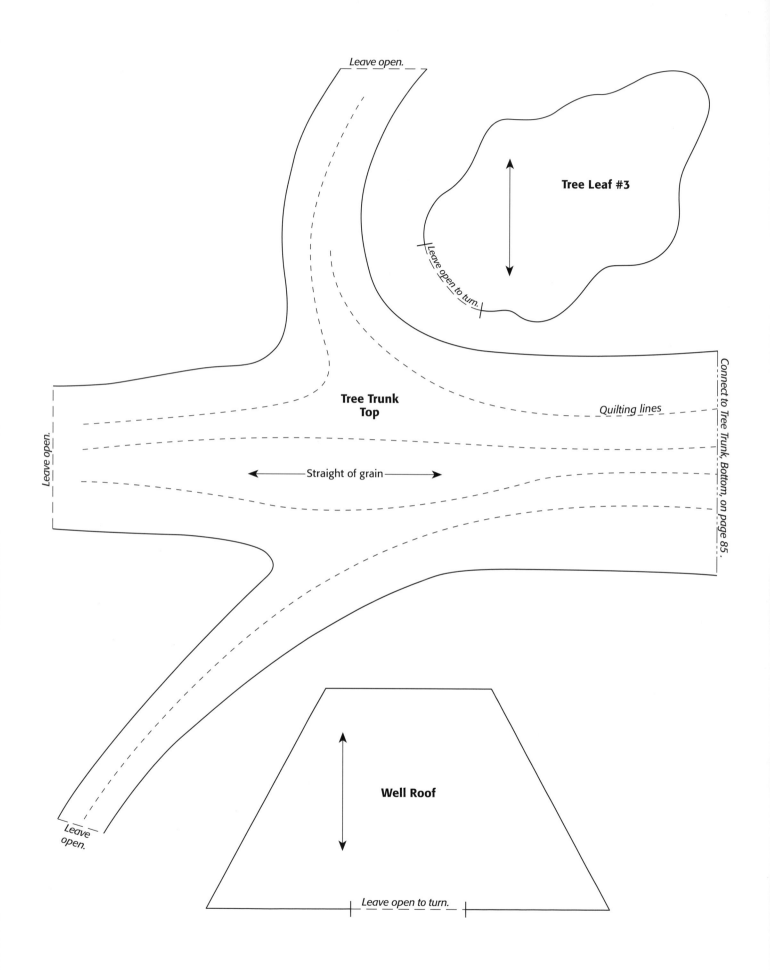

Leave open.

Tree Leaf #3

Leave open to turn.

Connect to Tree Trunk, Bottom, on page 85.

Tree Trunk Top

Quilting lines

Leave open.

←— Straight of grain —→

Leave open.

Well Roof

Leave open to turn.

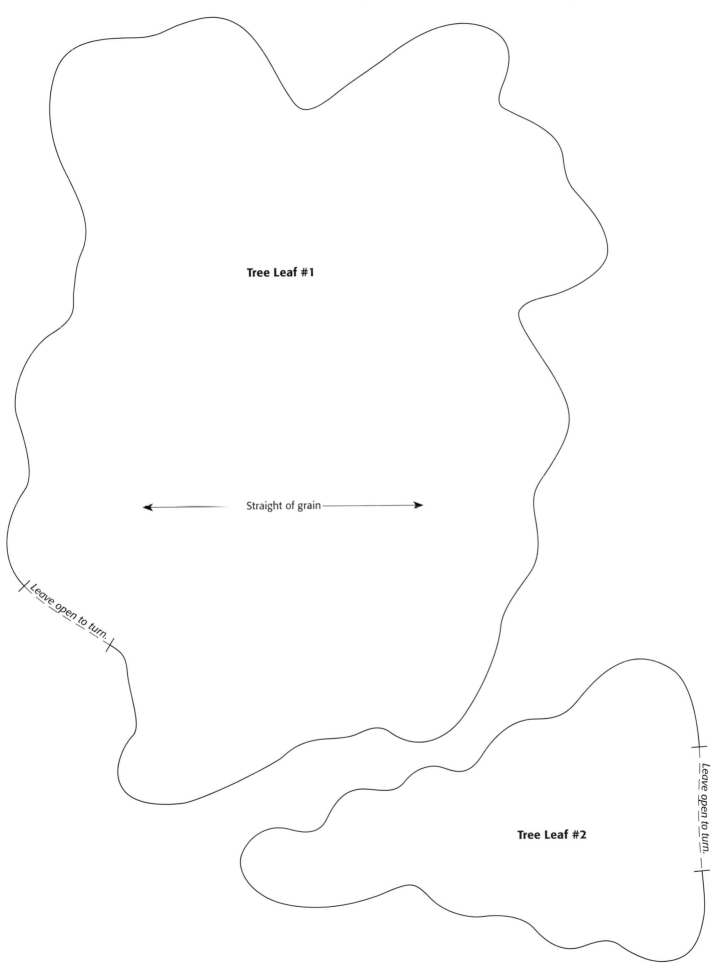

Tree Leaf #1

← Straight of grain →

Leave open to turn.

Tree Leaf #2

Leave open to turn.

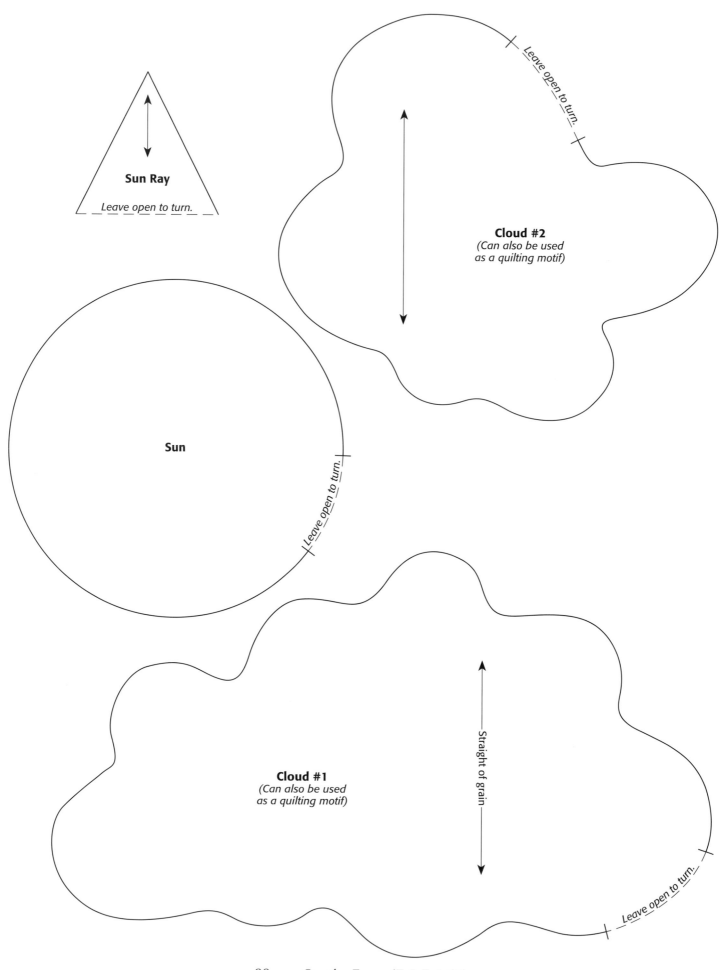

Sun Ray

Leave open to turn.

Sun

Cloud #2
*(Can also be used
as a quilting motif)*

Leave open to turn.

Cloud #1
*(Can also be used
as a quilting motif)*

Straight of grain

Leave open to turn.

Animal Train

Animal Train by Kristin Kolstad Addison, 2000, Førde, Norway.

Finished Size: 42¼" x 36½"
Dolls: animal train boy and girl
Two-Piece Animals: elephant, zebra, giraffe, lion
Moveable Flat Toys: moon, sun

Materials

42"-wide fabric

- ¾ yd. *total* of 6–8 assorted blue subtle prints (light to dark) for sky
- ⅔ yd. *total* assorted light green-print scraps for field
- ⅔ yd. green solid for field facing
- ⅜ yd. dark red subtle print for inner borders
- ⅝ yd. multicolor-checked fabric for outer borders
- ⅝ yd. black subtle print for binding and train track
- 1⅜ yds. fabric for backing
- Assorted scraps for engine and train wagons
- ⅜ yd. muslin for engine and train-wagon backs and facings
- Fabric scraps and assorted notions for dolls, animals, and moveable flat toys*
- 46" x 41" piece of batting
- Batting scraps for fixed items
- ⅔ yd. of ⅜"-wide black satin ribbon for train
- 12 large black buttons for train wheels
- 2 animal-face buttons for hanging moon and sun
- Tiny gold bell for train

* See instructions for specific doll, animal, or toy for fabrics and notions required.

Cutting

All measurements include ¼"-wide seam allowances.

From the assorted blue prints, cut a *total* of:
- 4 strips, each 2" x 21", for sky
- 4 strips, each 2½" x 21", for sky
- 4 strips, each 3" x 21", for sky
- 4 strips, each 3½" x 21", for sky

From the assorted light green-print scraps, cut a *total* of:
- 43 squares, each 4" x 4". Cut each square once diagonally to make 86 triangles for the field.

From the green solid, cut:
- 1 piece, 31¾" x 21", for field facing

From the dark red subtle print, cut:
- 4 strips, each 2" x 42", for inner borders

From the multicolored checked print, cut:
- 4 strips, each 4½" x 42", for outer borders

From the black subtle print, cut:
- 4 strips, each 3" x 42", for binding
- 1½"-wide bias strips to total 80", for train track**

** See "Cutting Accurate Strips," step 7 (page 9) and "Binding," step 1 (page 15) for guidance on cutting and piecing bias strips.

Note: *Refer to "Basic Quiltmaking Techniques" on pages 9–16 for guidance as needed with basic quilt construction.*

Assembling the Quilt

THE SKY is pieced from strips of varying widths, cut from a variety of different blue-print fabrics. The blues shade from dark on the left edge of the quilt to light on the right edge, suggesting the passage from night to day.

The field is constructed from 43 bias squares pieced from a variety of light green half-square triangles. It is faced, and it overlaps the sky background to form a large pocket on the front of the quilt.

1. Place the 2"- to 3½"-wide blue-print strips side by side in a random, visually pleasing arrangement, beginning with the darker strips and moving to the lighter as shown. Refer to the photo on page 89 and the illustration below for guidance as needed. Sew the strips together and press the seam allowances to one side. Trim this pieced background to measure 31¾" x 21".

Note: *Depending upon how you arrange the strips, you may have a few left over.*

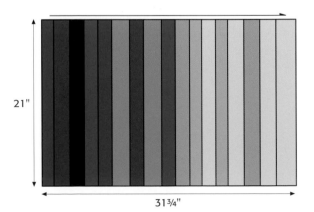

2. Pin light green triangles right sides together in scrappy pairs and sew along the long diagonal edge. Press the seam allowance toward the darker triangle. Make 43 bias squares.

Make 43.

3. Arrange the 43 bias squares randomly in 10 vertical rows, with each row containing the number of squares shown in the diagram below. Sew the squares into rows, and press the seams in opposite directions from row to row. Pin carefully to match the seams, and sew the rows together, aligning the bottom edges; press.

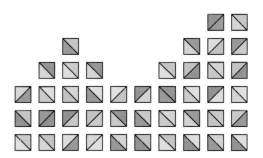

4. Place the field unit from step 3 and the 31¾" x 21" green facing piece right sides together, aligning the bottom raw edges. Press and pin the layers to secure them. With the pieced side on top, follow the top edge of the pieced unit to stitch the 2 layers together with a ¼"-wide seam. Leave the side and bottom edges open. Remove the pins.

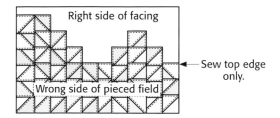

5. Clip the outer corners, and notch the inner corners as necessary before turning the faced unit right side out; press. Quilt ¼" from the edge along the stitched (top) edge of the field. Repin the layers.

6. Place the sky unit from step 1 right side up on your work surface. Position the faced field unit right side up, with the finished (staggered) edge overlapping the bottom edge of the sky. Adjust the placement as necessary so the entire piece measures 26" from top to bottom. Pin (or thread-baste) the layers to secure them.

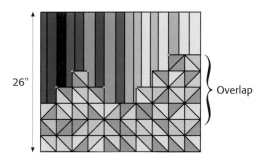

7. Measure the quilt through its horizontal center. Cut two 2" x 42" dark red inner border strips to that measurement and sew them to the top and bottom of the quilt. Press the seams toward the borders.

8. Measure the quilt through its vertical center, including the borders just added. Trim the remaining two 2" x 42" dark red inner border strips to opposite sides of the quilt; press.

9. Repeat steps 5 and 6 to measure, trim, and sew the 4½" x 42" multicolored checked outer border strips to the top, bottom, and sides of the quilt; press.

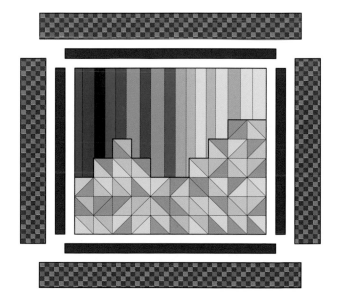

Layering, Quilting, and Binding

1. Center and layer the quilt top over the batting and backing; baste.

2. Quilt as desired. Since the quilt has so many layers, I recommend machine quilting. Leave some areas of the field unquilted so the top edges remain open as pockets for the dolls and animals. Tack random corners along the top edge of the field through all layers to secure.

Suggested Quilting Plan

3. Use the 3" x 42" black subtle-print strips to make the binding. Sew the binding to the quilt. Trim the batting and backing even with the edges of the quilt top. Blindstitch to secure the binding

4. Make a label and attach it to your quilt.

Making the Track and Train

THE ANIMAL train consists of an engine (A) and 5 wagons (B–F) traveling down a bias-strip track.

The Track

1. Refer to "Binding," step 1 (page 15). Sew the 1½"-wide black subtle-print bias strips together end to end to make a single 80"-long bias strip. Fold the strip lengthwise, matching the long raw edges. Stitch ½" from the folded edge all along the length of the strip.

2. Center the seam on the underside and press the strip flat. (A ½"-wide bias press bar and touch of spray starch will help with this step.)

3. Position and pin the train track, seam side down, to the quilt. Refer to the photo on page 89 for guidance as needed. Use black thread and a straight, zigzag, or other stitch to machine sew the track to the quilt. Place the track no lower than the bottom edge of the sky.

Engine (A)

1. Trace the engine pattern on page 94 onto your preferred template material. Cut out template.

2. You'll need to cut 4 fabric pieces and 1 piece of thin batting for the engine. Place the template on the wrong side of a black subtle-print scrap, noting the grain-line markings. Trace around the outside edge of the pattern (*not the center opening!*) with a sharp pencil. Cut out the piece, adding a ¼" seam allowance. Repeat to trace and cut 1 identical piece from a scrap of muslin (for the backing). In addition, trace and cut 1 piece minus the chimney from

muslin (for the front facing), an orange plaid scrap (for the see-through window), and a scrap of thin batting.

3. Pin the black subtle-print engine shape and the muslin front facing piece (minus the chimney) right sides together. Place the template over the black fabric and trace the center opening onto the fabric. Remove the template and sew directly on the line with matching thread, all around the center opening. Cut out the circle through all layers, leaving a ¼"-wide seam allowance. Clip the seam allowances, turn the piece right side out through the opening; press.

4. Layer the unit from step 3 (right side up), the muslin backing piece, the batting, and the orange plaid piece (right side up). Pin the layers, and then sew around the outside edge of the engine unit on the drawn line. Leave a small opening for turning.

5. Clip the corners as needed to reduce bulk. Turn the piece right side out so that the black subtle-print unit is on top with the orange plaid peeking through; press. Set the engine aside for now.

Train Wagons C and F

Follow the instructions for the engine (page 92) using the patterns for wagons C (page 94) and F (page 95). I used a black-print scrap for the front of wagon C, muslin for the front facing and backing, and a yellow-striped scrap for the see-through window layer. For wagon F, I used a bright orange print for the front, muslin for the front facing and backing, and a yellow-checked scrap for the window layer.

Train Wagons B, D, and E

Follow the instructions for the basic moveable flat toy (page 45), steps 1–5, using the pattern on page 94 for wagon B and on page 95 for wagon D and wagon E. I combined red-plaid and yellow-checked scraps for the front of wagon B, 2 orange-plaid scraps for the front of wagon D, and used a black novelty print for the front of wagon E. I used muslin as the backing for all 3 pieces.

Attaching the Train

1. Measure the diameter of the buttons you plan to use for wheels and position the engine and wagons that same measurement from the train track. Refer to the photo on page 92 for guidance as necessary. Pin the train pieces to the quilt along their top edges.

2. Run a 24" length of ⅜"-wide ribbon underneath the train pieces to "connect" them; pin it in place.

3. Use matching thread to hand stitch the engine and train wagons to the quilt along their side and bottom edges. Leave the top edges open so the pieces can be used as pockets for the dolls and animals.

> ## Tip
> **Catch all layers of the quilt so the pieces remain intact as children play with them.**

4. Use matching thread to sew the button wheels to the quilt. Sew 3 wheels to the engine; 2 each to wagons B, C, D, and F; and 1 to wagon E. Add a tiny gold bell to the top of the engine chimney. Just remember to attach all buttons and trinkets securely; this quilt is made for children (ages 3 and older) to play with.

Making the Dolls, Animals, and Moveable Toys

1. Using the photo on page 89 for guidance, sew 2 animal-face buttons to the quilt for attaching the moon and sun.

2. Refer to the instructions and photos indicated by page number, and use the appropriate fabrics, scraps, and notions to make the following dolls and toys:

   • Sun (page 48) and moon (page 49). Attach these items by buttoning them to the quilt as desired with the animal-faced buttons.

   • One each of the train boy and girl dolls (page 23). Place each doll in the pocket of a train wagon.

   • One each of the elephant (page 30), zebra (page 30), giraffe (page 31), and lion (page 31). Insert the animals in various train wagons.

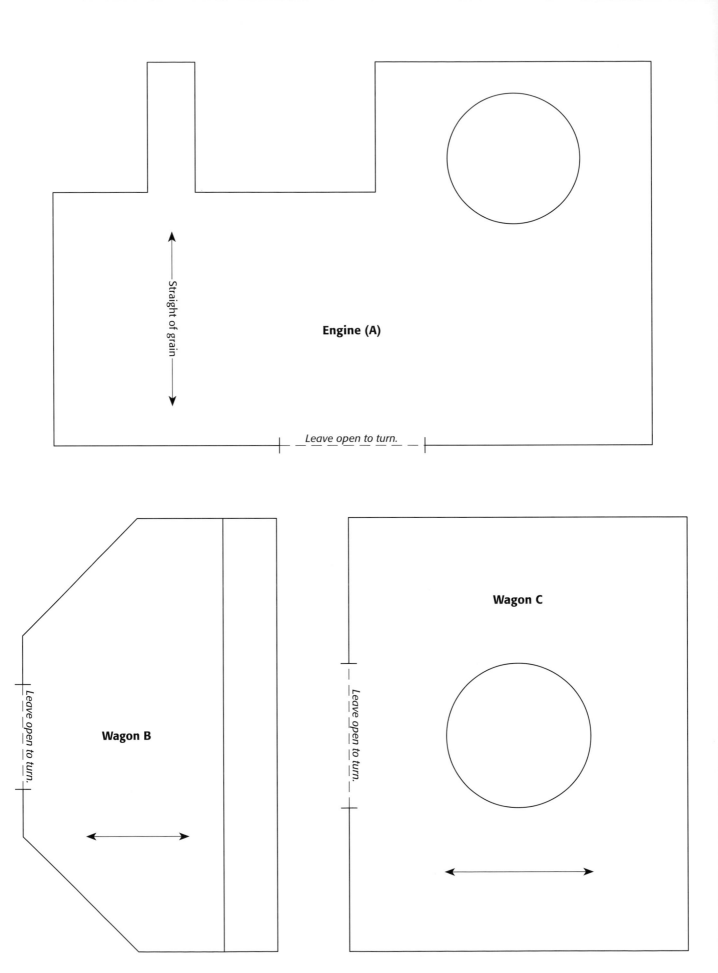

Engine (A)

Straight of grain

Leave open to turn.

Wagon B

Leave open to turn.

Wagon C

Leave open to turn.

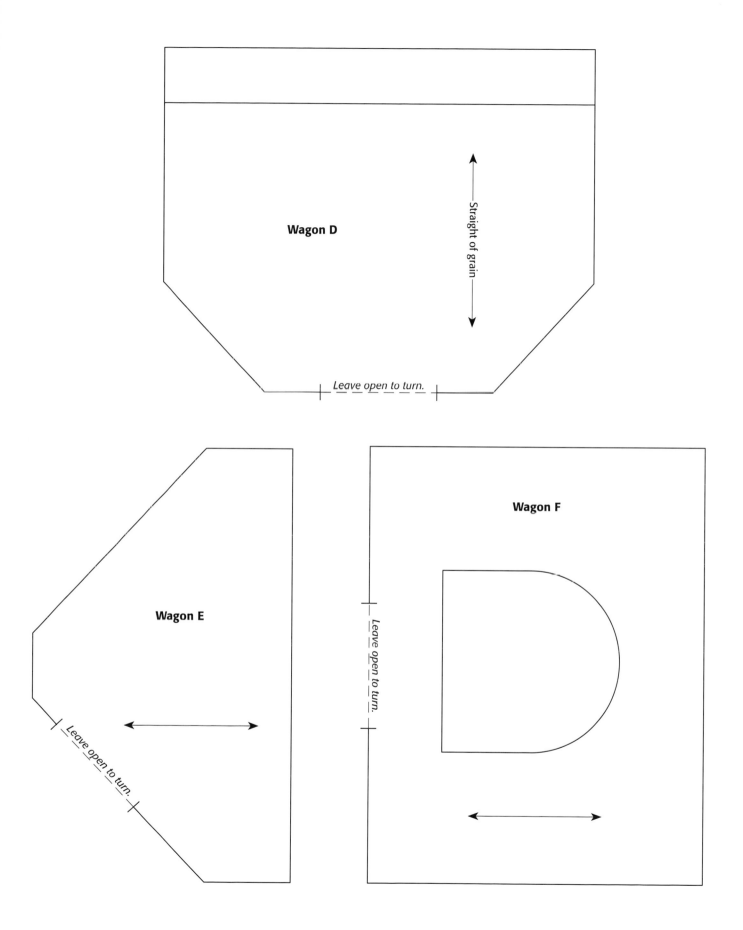

Wagon D

Straight of grain

Leave open to turn.

Wagon E

Leave open to turn.

Wagon F

Leave open to turn.

Sleepover Picnic

Sleepover Picnic by Kristin Kolstad Addison, 2000, Førde, Norway.

Finished quilt size: 48½" x 50"
Dolls: sleepover girls #1 through #6, mini doll
One-Piece Animals: teddy bear, rabbit, dragon
Moveable Flat Toys: moon, campfire
Mini-Quilt Sleeping Bags: Amish, Durham, cathedral window (small and large), bargello (almost!), and scrap

Materials

42"-wide fabric

- ¼ yd. *each* of 7 assorted blue prints (light to dark) for sky and tree backgrounds
- 1 yd. medium green print for forest floor and tree backgrounds
- ¾ yd. total assorted dark green scraps for trees
- ¼ yd. dark red subtle print #1 for inner borders
- ¾ yd. medium red print for outer borders
- ½ yd. dark red subtle print #2 for binding
- 3⅛ yds. fabric for backing
- ⅓ yd. blue-and-turquoise mottled print for lake
- 53" x 54" piece of batting
- 15–20 utility and theme-related buttons for hanging toys and sleeping bags and for extra decoration
- Fabric scraps and assorted notions for dolls, animals, moveable flat toys, and mini-quilt sleeping bags*

* *See instructions for specific doll, animal, toy, or mini quilt for fabrics and notions required.*

Cutting

MAKE TEMPLATES for pieces A through K by transferring the patterns on pages 109–110 onto your preferred template material. Cut out the template. Label each template with the appropriate letter and grain-line arrow. With the exception of loose branches L–M (which don't require them), all templates and cutting measurements include ¼"-wide seam allowances.

From *each* of the assorted blue prints, cut:
- 1 strip, 2½" x 42" (total 7 strips). Subcut each strip into 16 squares, each 2½" x 2½" (total 112 squares), for sky.

From the assorted blue prints, cut a *total* of: **
- 4 piece B and 4 B reverse, for tree backgrounds
- 4 piece D and 4 D reverse, for tree backgrounds
- 4 piece F and 4 F reverse, for tree backgrounds
- 4 piece H and 4 H reverse, for tree backgrounds
- 4 piece J, for tree backgrounds
- 4 piece K and 4 K reverse, for tree backgrounds

From the medium green print, cut:
- 4 squares, each 2½" x 2½", for forest floor (in sky-unit 4)
- 1 piece, 8½" x 5½", for forest floor (unit 6)
- 1 piece, 8½" x 6", for forest floor (unit 7)
- 1 piece, 8½" x 11", for forest floor (unit 8)
- 1 piece, 8½" x 4½", for forest floor (unit 9)
- 1 piece, 8½" x 25", for forest floor (unit 10)
- 2 pieces, 8½" x 19", for forest floor (units 11 and 12)
- 2 piece B and 2 B reverse, for tree backgrounds
- 2 piece D and 2 D reverse, for tree backgrounds
- 2 piece F and 2 F reverse, for tree backgrounds
- 2 piece H and 2 H reverse, for tree backgrounds
- 2 piece J, for tree backgrounds
- 2 piece K and 2 K reverse, for tree backgrounds

From the assorted dark green scraps, cut a *total* of:
- 6 each of pieces A, C, E, G, and I, for trees
- 18 piece L, each 1¾" x 3", for loose branches
- 12 piece M, each 3" x 4", for loose branches
- 6 piece N, each 4½" x 5½", for loose branches

From the dark red subtle print #1, cut:
- 4 strips, each 1½" x 42", for inner border

From the medium red print, cut:
- 5 strips, each 4½" x 42", for outer border

From the dark red subtle print #2, cut:
- 5 strips, each 3" x 42", for binding

From the blue-and-turquoise mottled print, cut:
- 1 strip, 10" x 42", for the lake

** *Cut the blue background pieces for 1 tree from dark blue print scraps, 2 from medium blue print scraps, and 1 from light blue print scraps. Refer to the photo on page 96 for guidance as needed.*

Note: *Refer to "Basic Quiltmaking Techniques" on pages 9–16 for guidance as needed.*

Piecing the Sky

1. Refer to the photo on page 96 and the assembly diagram on page 99. Use your design wall or other large flat surface to arrange the 2½" assorted blue and green squares to make the 5 pieced sky units, beginning with the darker squares (unit 1) and moving to the lighter squares (unit 5) as shown.

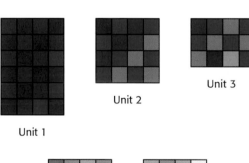

Unit 1

Unit 2

Unit 3

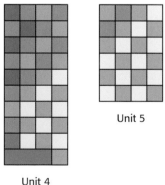

Unit 4

Unit 5

2. Referring to "Quick Chain Piecing" on page 10, sew the squares into units 1 through 5; press. Set the individual units aside for now.

Tree Blocks

YOU'LL NEED to make 6 tree blocks for this quilt. Each tree finishes 8" x 8" and is pieced from a variety of green-print scraps. Follow the steps below to make each tree block, using either similarly-valued all blue or all green background (B, D, F, H, and K, regular and reversed, plus J) pieces. Refer to the block diagram on page 99 as needed.

1. With right sides together and diagonal edges aligned, sew a piece A between a B regular and B reverse piece. Press the seams toward the tree pieces. Repeat to sew a piece C between a piece D regular and D reverse, a piece E between a piece F regular and F reverse, and a piece G between a piece H regular and H reverse.

2. Sew pieces I and J together, pivoting as shown; press.

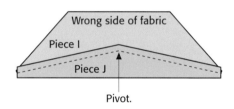

Wrong side of fabric

Piece I

Piece J

Pivot.

3. Finish the unit by sewing a piece K and K reverse to each short side as shown in the block diagram. Do not sew rows together.

4. To make the loose branches, fold each of the dark green print loose branch pieces in half, right sides together, aligning the shorter edges; press. Stitch and trim as shown. Turn the branches right side out.

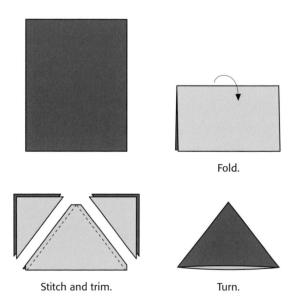

Fold.

Stitch and trim.

Turn.

5. Refer to the block diagram below and lay out the rows. Sew the rows together, inserting the loose branches (pieces L, M, and N), fold side down, in the seams as shown; press.

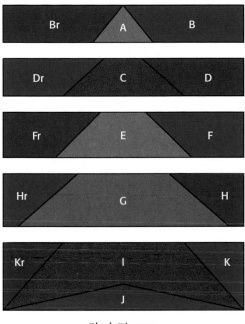

Block Diagram

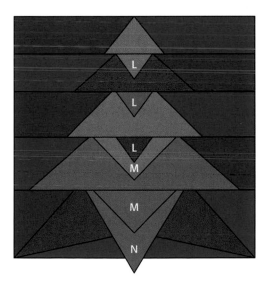

Assembling the Quilt Top

1. Refer to the assembly diagram below and the photo on page 96. Arrange the sky units (1–5), the trees, and the green-print forest-floor strips (6–12) as shown. Sew the units into vertical rows and press the seam allowances in opposite directions from row to row. Sew the vertical rows together and press.

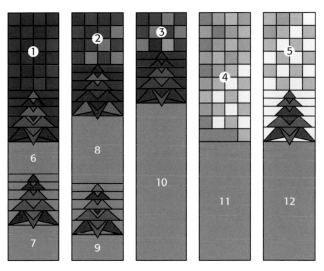

Assembly Diagram

2. Measure the quilt through its horizontal center. Cut two 1½" x 42" dark red subtle print #1 inner border strips to that measurement and sew them to the top and bottom of the quilt. Press the seams toward the borders.

3. Measure the quilt through its vertical center, including the borders just added. Trim the remaining 1½" x 42" dark red subtle print #1 inner border strips and sew them to opposite sides of the quilt; press.

4. Sew the 4½" x 42" medium red print outer border strips end to end to make a continuous 4½"-wide border. Measure the quilt through its horizontal center, and cut 2 borders to that measurement. Sew the borders to the top and bottom of the quilt, and press the seams toward the outer borders.

5. Measure the quilt through its vertical center, including the borders just added. Cut 2 borders to that measurement from the remaining pieced border strip and sew them to opposite sides of the quilt; press.

Layering, Quilting, and Binding

1. Divide the backing fabric crosswise into 2 equal panels of approximately 56" each. Remove the selvages and join the pieces to make a single backing panel.

2. Position the backing so that the seam runs vertically. Center and layer the quilt top and the batting over the backing; baste.

3. Quilt as desired.

4. Use the 3" x 42" dark red subtle-print #2 strips to make the binding. Sew the binding to the quilt. Trim the batting and backing even with the edges of the quilt top. Blindstitch to secure the binding.

5. Make a label and attach it to your quilt.

Suggested Quilting Plan

Making the Fixed Items

THERE ARE 2 fixed items on this quilt: a cave that doubles as a pocket, and a dimensional lake.

Cave

1. Follow the instructions for the basic moveable flat toy, steps 1 through 5, (page 45). Use the cave pattern on page 111 and matching medium dark green scraps for the front and the backing. Omit the batting.

2. Refer to the photo on page 96, and use matching thread and an invisible stitch to sew the cave to the quilt, leaving one end open as indicated on the pattern to make a pocket.

Lake

1. Refer to the photo on page 96, and the detail above. Crumple and drape the 10" x 42" piece of blue-and-turquoise-print fabric in the lower-right corner of the quilt, overhanging the borders, to form a wavy, dimensional lake. Pin the lake to the quilt.

2. Use matching thread and an invisible stitch to hand-appliqué the lake to the quilt, turning under all raw edges as you sew.

3. Add some tacking stitches to the lake, under the folds, to further secure it to the quilt.

Making the Dolls, Animals, Moveable Toys, and Mini-Quilt Sleeping Bags

1. Using the photo on page 96 for guidance, sew 15–20 assorted utility and theme-related buttons to the quilt for decoration and for attaching the moon, animals, and mini-sleeping bags. Include frogs and fish in the pond, hearts, birds, butterflies, and flowers for detail and whimsy. Remember to attach all buttons and trinkets securely; this quilt is made for children to play with (keep away from children under age 3).

2. Refer to the instructions and photos indicated by page number and use the appropriate fabrics, scraps, and notions to make the following dolls and toys:

   - Moon (page 49) and campfire (page 49). Attach the moon by buttoning it to the quilt. Sew the remaining half of the campfire snap to the quilt and fasten the fire in place.

   - One each of sleepover girl #1 through #6 (pages 24–27) and the mini doll (page 27). Set the dolls aside.

   - One each of the teddy bear (page 38), rabbit (page 39), and dragon (page 39). Attach the rabbit and dragon by buttoning them to the quilt as desired. Put the teddy bear in the cave.

   - One each of the following mini quilts: Amish (page 102), Durham (page 104), small cathedral window (page 104), large cathedral window (page 105), bargello (almost!) (page 107), and scrap (pages 108). Use each of the mini quilts to construct a sleeping bag as instructed on page 108. Attach the sleeping bags by buttoning them to the quilt as desired.

The Miniature Quilts

EACH OF THE dolls at the "Sleepover Picnic" has her very own sleeping bag to sleep in. The top layer of each sleeping bag is a different miniature quilt. I've given you the instructions for making each mini quilt separately, and then included the directions for making the sleeping bags. Attach the sleeping bags by buttoning them to the quilt as desired.

Amish Mini Quilt

Finished Size: 4" x 4"

You'll need: scraps of black, yellow, orange, and red solids; scraps of batting and backing.

All cut measurements include ¼"-wide seam allowances.

From black solid scraps, cut:
- 1 square, 1" x 1", for center square
- 1 square, 2" x 2". Cut square twice diagonally to make 4 small triangles for background.
- 1 square 3¼" x 3¼". Cut square twice diagonally to make 4 large triangles for background.
- 2 strips, each ¾" x 4", for the outer border
- 2 strips, each ¾" x 4½", for the outer border

From yellow solid scraps, cut:
- 4 pieces, each ¾" x 1", for center square

From orange solid scraps, cut:
- 4 squares, each ¾" x ¾", for center square
- 4 pieces, each ¾" x 2", for on-point square

From red solid scraps, cut:
- 4 squares, each ¾" x ¾", for on-point square
- 2 strips, each ¾" x 3⅜", for inner border
- 2 strips, each ¾" x 4", for inner border

From both the batting and backing fabric, cut:
- 1 square, each 4½" x 4½"

Constructing the Quilt

Note: *Refer to "Basic Quiltmaking Techniques" on pages 9–16 for guidance as needed.*

1. Sew a ¾" x 1" yellow piece to opposite sides of the 1" black square. Press seams toward the black square.

2. Sew a ¾" orange square to opposite short ends of each remaining ¾" x 1" yellow strip. Press seams toward the orange squares.

3. Sew the unit from step 1 between the 2 units from step 2 as shown. Press seams toward the center unit.

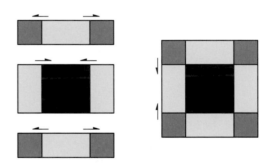

4. Sew the long side of a small black triangle to 2 opposite sides of the unit from step 3. Press seams toward the triangles. Repeat to add the remaining small black triangles; press.

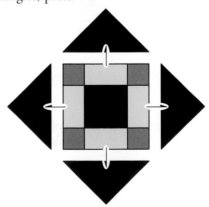

5. Sew a ¾" x 2" orange strip to opposite sides of the unit from step 4. Press seams toward the orange strips.

6. Sew a ¾" red square to opposite short ends of each remaining ¾" x 2" orange strip. Press seams toward the orange strips.

7. Sew the unit from step 4 between the 2 units from step 6 as shown. Press seams toward the center unit.

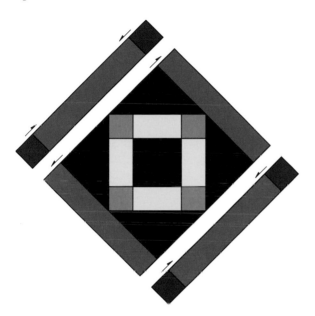

8. Sew the long side of a large black triangle to 2 opposite sides of the unit from step 7. Press seams toward the triangles. Repeat to add the remaining large black triangles; press.

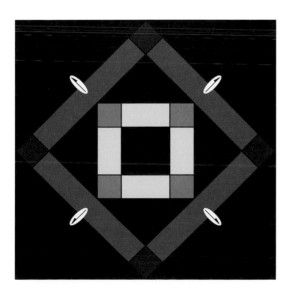

9. Sew ¾" x 3⅜" red borders to opposite sides of the quilt, and trim as necessary. Press the seams toward the borders. Sew the ¾" x 4" red borders to the remaining 2 sides, and press. Repeat to sew the ¾" x 4" and ¾" x 4½" black borders to the quilt; press.

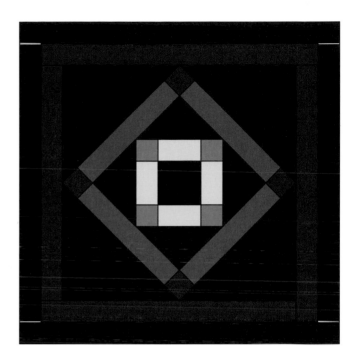

10. Layer the batting, the quilt top (right side up), and the backing (wrong side up), and pin. Sew around the perimeter with a ¼"-wide seam, leaving a small opening in one end for turning. Trim all corners, turn the unit right side out, and press. Close by hand with a blind or ladder stitch, turning the seam allowance in as you sew.

11. Quilt as desired. The sample is quilted alongside the seam (in the ditch) around each shape.

Durham Mini Quilt

Quilting Pattern

Finished size: 4" x 4"

You'll need: scraps of white silk, backing fabric, and batting.

All cut measurements include ¼"-wide seam allowances.

From white silk, cut:
- 1 square, 4½" x 4½", for quilt top

From backing fabric, cut:
- 1 square, 4½" x 4½"

From batting, cut:
- 1 square, 4½" x 4½"

Constructing the Quilt

Note: *Refer to "Basic Quiltmaking Techniques" on pages 9–16 for guidance as needed.*

1. Use a removable marker (and a lightbox, if necessary) to transfer the quilting pattern (right) to the right side of the 4½" white silk square.

2. Layer the batting, the 4½" silk square (marked side up), and the backing (wrong side up), and pin. Sew around the perimeter with a ¼"-wide seam, leaving a small opening in one end for turning. Trim all corners and turn the unit right side out. Close by hand with a blind or ladder stitch, turning the seam allowance in as you sew.

3. Quilt in the thread color of your choice.

Cathedral Window Mini Quilt (Small)

Finished size: 4" x 4"

You'll need: scrap of navy fabric, scraps of 9 prints, backing fabric, and batting.

All cut measurements include ¼"-wide seam allowances.

From the navy solid, cut:
- 9 squares, each 3" x 3", for blocks

From *each* of 9 different print scraps, cut:
- 1 square, ½" x ½", for blocks

From both the batting and the backing fabric, cut:
- 1 square, each 4½" x 4½"

Constructing the Quilt

Note: *Refer to "Basic Quiltmaking Techniques" on pages 9–16 for guidance as needed.*

1. Fold each 3" navy square in half twice as shown.

2. Unfold a square. Working clockwise around the square, fold each crease mark toward the next parallel raw edge, pinning the crease ⅜" from the raw edge as shown. A little "peak" will form in the center of the square. Press the peak, and you will see a new, smaller square appear on the diagonals of the original square. The navy square should now measure 1⅞" x 1⅞".

Press folds.

3. Place a ½" print square over the new folded square. If necessary, trim the print square so that it is slightly smaller than the folded square. Roll the edges of the folded square over the raw edges of the print square, and hand tack the rolled edge in place with matching thread and tiny invisible stitches. Stop stitching about ⅛" from each corner.

½" print square

Roll and tack the
folded navy square.

4. Repeat steps 2 and 3 to make the remaining 8 blocks.

5. Sew the blocks into 3 rows of 3 blocks each, removing the pins as you go. Press the seams open. Sew the 3 rows together, matching the seams, and press.

6. Layer the batting, the quilt top (right side up), and the backing (wrong side up), and pin. Sew around the perimeter with a ¼"-wide seam, leaving a small opening in one end for turning. Trim all corners, turn the unit right side out, and press. Close by hand with a blind or ladder stitch, turning the seam allowance in as you sew.

7. Quilt as desired. The sample is quilted alongside the seams (in the ditch) joining the blocks.

Cathedral Window Mini Quilt (Large)

Finished size: 4" x 4"

You'll need: scraps of light print and dark print.

All cut measurements include ¼"-wide seam allowances.

From the light print, cut:
- 4 squares, each 4½" x 4½", for blocks

From the dark contrasting print, cut:
- 4 squares, each 1" x 1", for blocks

Constructing the Quilt

1. Fold one 4½" light-print square on both diagonals to find its center, pressing each fold lightly with the tip of the iron. Unfold the creased square and lay it wrong side up. Fold a ¼"-wide hem over to the wrong side on each edge of the square; press.

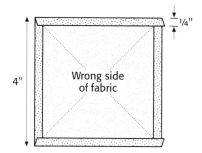

2. Fold each corner inward so that all 4 meet in the center of the square; press.

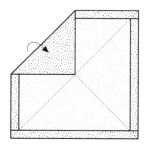 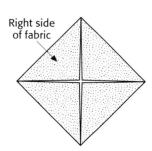

Tip

It is very important that the new outer corners be as square as possible, even if it means the inner corners don't meet exactly in the center.

---

3. Repeat step 2 to fold the corners to the center a second time. Keep the new outer corners as square as possible, but this time the center *must be perfect*. Make a few tacking stitches in the center to keep the corners in place. Use matching colored thread, be sure to catch all layers, and fasten on the back of the square. The square should now measure 2".

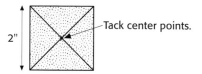

4. Repeat steps 1 through 3 to make the remaining 3 blocks.

5. Whipstitch the blocks together in 2 rows of 2 blocks each. Whipstitch the 2 rows together, carefully matching the seams.

6. Pin a 1" dark square over the seam line between 2 blocks. Trim ⅛" from all sides of the 1" square. Roll one folded edge of an adjacent square over the raw edge of the trimmed dark square. Beginning ¼" from the corner, sew the rolled edge in place with matching thread and tiny stitches, forming a curve as you go. End ¼" from the corner on the opposite end of the curve. Repeat for the remaining 3 sides and the remaining 3 dark squares.

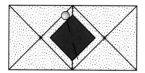

Pin a 1" square
over seam line.

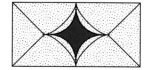

Roll edges and stitch.

7. Refer to the photo on page 105, and—if you'd like—sew 5 tiny silk flowers as shown.

Bargello (Almost!) Mini Quilt

Finished size: 4" x 4"

You'll need: scraps of 7 different fabrics, backing fabric, and batting.

All cut measurements include ¼"-wide seam allowances.

From *each* of 7 different print fabrics, cut:

1 strip, each 1½" x 8", for piecing

From both the batting and backing fabric, cut:

1 square, each 4½" x 4½"

Constructing the Quilt

Note: *Refer to "Basic Quiltmaking Techniques" on pages 9–16 for guidance as needed.*

1. With right sides together and long raw edges aligned, sew the 1½" x 8" strips together in a random, visually pleasing arrangement. Press the seams to one side.

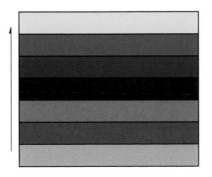

2. Fold the new fabric unit right sides together, aligning the long raw edges, and sew a ¼"-wide seam to make a tube.

3. Use a rotary cutter to cut 8 to 10 slices, ranging in width from ¾" to 1½" wide.

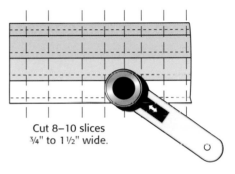

Cut 8–10 slices
¾" to 1 ½" wide.

4. Use scissors to cut the strips open at different places on the tube.

   Refer to the photo at left and lay the strips side by side to make a pleasing, staggered arrangement. Sew the rows together and press the seams as desired. Trim the finished piece to a 4½" x 4½" square.

5. Layer the batting, the quilt top (right side up), and the backing (wrong side up), and pin. Sew around the perimeter with a ¼"-wide seam, leaving a small opening in one end for turning. Trim all corners, turn the unit right side out, and press. Close by hand with a blind or ladder stitch, turning the seam allowance in as you sew.

6. Quilt as desired. The sample is quilted in zigzag lines across the top, emphasizing the staggered rows.

Mini Scrap Quilt

You'll need: a variety of print scraps, scrap of flannel solid, scraps of backing fabric and batting.

All cut measurements include ¼"-wide seam allowances.

From the variety of different print scraps, cut a total of:
- 16 squares, each 1¼" x 1¼", for piecing

From the complementary flannel solid, cut:
- 2 strips, each 1¼" x 3½", for border
- 2 strips, each 1¼" x 4½", for border

From both the batting and backing fabric, cut:
- 1 square, each 4½" x 4½"

Constructing the Quilt

Note: *Refer to "Basic Quiltmaking Techniques" on pages 9–16 for guidance as needed.*

1. Refer to the photo above and arrange the sixteen 1¼" squares in a pleasing arrangement of 4 rows of 4 squares each. Sew the squares into rows. Press the seam allowances in opposite directions from row to

row. Sew the rows together and press as desired.

2. Sew a 1" x 3½" flannel border to the top and bottom of the quilt. Press the seams toward the borders. Sew the 1" x 4½" flannel borders to the remaining 2 sides; press.

3. Layer the batting, the quilt top (right side up), and the backing (wrong side up), and pin. Sew around the perimeter with a ¼"-wide seam, leaving a small opening in one end for turning. Trim all corners, turn the unit right side out, and press. Close by hand with a blind or ladder stitch, turning the seam allowance in as you sew.

4. Quilt as desired. The sample is quilted alongside the seams (in the ditch) between each square.

Sleeping Bag

You'll need: two 4½" x 5¾" strips of fabric in colors to match the quilt, one 4½" x 5¾" strip of batting.

To make each quilt into a sleeping bag:

1. Layer the fabric strips right sides together over the batting, and sew around the perimeter with a ¼"-wide seam. Leave a small opening in one short end for turning. Trim all corners and turn the unit right side out; press.

2. Close the opening with a blind or ladder stitch, turning the seam allowance to the inside as you stitch.

3. Select a button and make a buttonhole to fit in the center of the backing unit. (The buttonhole goes through all 3 layers.)

4. Layer the quilt top (right side up) over the sleeping-bag back (right side up), aligning the bottom and side edges. Use matching thread and a tiny whip-stitch to sew the quilt to the sleeping-bag back on the bottom and side edges.

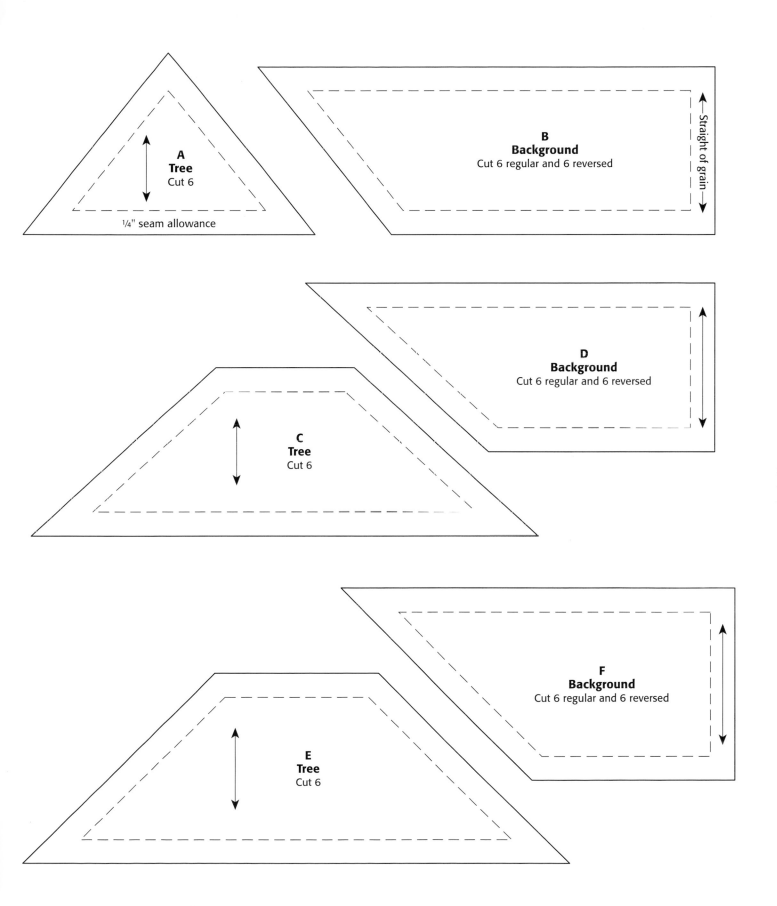

A
Tree
Cut 6

¼" seam allowance

B
Background
Cut 6 regular and 6 reversed

Straight of grain

D
Background
Cut 6 regular and 6 reversed

C
Tree
Cut 6

F
Background
Cut 6 regular and 6 reversed

E
Tree
Cut 6

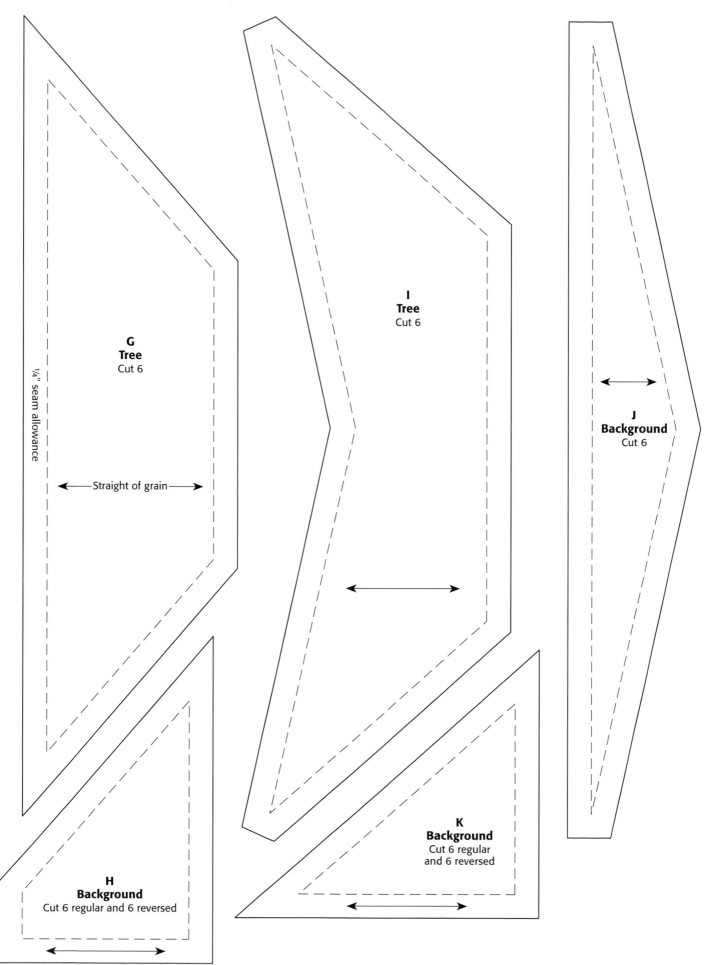

G
Tree
Cut 6

¼" seam allowance

←——— Straight of grain ———→

I
Tree
Cut 6

J
Background
Cut 6

H
Background
Cut 6 regular and 6 reversed

K
Background
Cut 6 regular
and 6 reversed

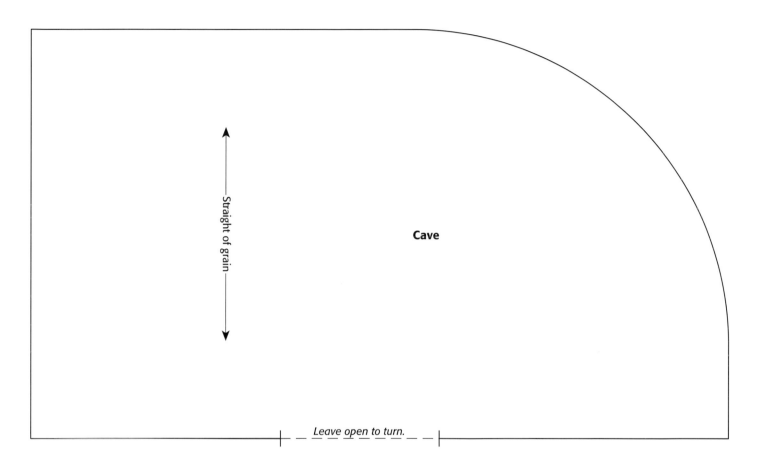

Straight of grain

Cave

Leave open to turn.

About the Author

Kristin Kolstad Addison has enjoyed handcraft, and especially sewing, all her life. In 1992 she started her first quilt. In 1994 she attended her first quilt class, and in 1996 she taught her first beginner class. She has been teaching and quilting ever since.

Kristin sews while her children play. Sharing their playroom inspires her to make quilts and toys for her daughters and also led her to design play quilts.

Kristin lives in a small town called Førde on the beautiful west coast of Norway with her husband, Thomas, her three girls, seven and three years old, and their very active dog.